REIKI FOR BEGINNERS

The Step-by-Step Guide to Unlock Reiki Self-Healing and Aura Cleansing Secrets for Deep Healing, Peace of Mind, and Spiritual Growth

Rohit Sahu

Copyright © 2021 Rohit Sahu

All rights reserved. No part of this publication may be reproduced, distributed, or transmitted in any form or by any means, including photocopying, recording, or other electronic or mechanical methods, without the prior written permission of the publisher, except in the case of brief quotations embodied in critical reviews and certain other non-commercial uses permitted by copyright law. For permission requests, write to the publisher at the email below.

Published by: Rohit Sahu
Contact: rohit@rohitsahu.net
Published Worldwide

CONTENTS

Title Page
Copyright
Introduction — 2
Basics, History, and Principles of Reiki — 7
Reiki's Foundational Pillars — 17
Reiki Advantages — 24
The Energy Architecture of the Body — 36
How Reiki Can Help with Kundalini Awakening? — 47
The Meridians in Your Body — 51
Aura Cleansing and Reiki — 59
Treating Energy Blocks in Your Mind and Body — 70
Step-by-Step Reiki Healing — 83
Reiki Symbols for Distance Healing — 112
Healing Others — 123
Healing with Crystals — 130
Tips to Boost Your Reiki Growth — 140
Reiki's Most Common FAQs and Myths — 151
Closing Words — 163
Author Note — 164
Here's Your FREE GIFT!! — 167
Books By This Author — 170

With this application-focused reference book, unveil the fundamental techniques of energy healing essential to recover from physical, emotional, and mental ailments. It's an all-in-one resource for improving your skills in Reiki Healing, Aura Cleansing, Symbol Activations, Distance Healing, Crystal Healing, and more...

INTRODUCTION

Have you ever sensed the calming vibe of another person? It may feel warm, comforting, and very therapeutic. And have you ever felt the same energy inside yourself, whether in times of peace or during yoga practice—when you can sense your own life force whirling within you? Reiki works similarly. It is a kind of energy healing that goes back to the late 1800s, yet its advantages easily apply to the modern world.

Reiki (霊気) is a complementary form of energy healing that originated in Japan. It is a gentle but strong hands-on energy healing technique that has grown in popularity over the past century, not just among Western bodyworkers and massage therapists, but also among medical experts who can confirm its healing potential.

Reiki is sometimes known as 'palm healing or hands-on healing.' "Reiki" is a Japanese term that means 'mysterious atmosphere, amazing sign.' It is derived from the Japanese terms "Rei," which means universal, and "Ki/Chi," which means life force.

It was founded by a Japanese Buddhist called Mikao Usui and is based on the basic spiritual concept that all people have energy fields, or life energies, which keep us alive. That we are all governed by the same unseen life force, which regulates our physical, mental, and emotional health. When energy flows freely, we may access undiscovered sources of power. But when it runs into blockages (often said to be caused by negative thinking, unhealed trauma, or stress overload), we function at a suboptimal level.

Reiki is based on the idea that disrupting it may cause health problems. Physical, mental, and emotional problems may arise if this energy is depleted or obstructed, according to the discipline.

Reiki therapy seeks to correct these disturbances and the resulting symptoms. Energy healing, like acupuncture or acupressure, seeks to improve the flow of energy and eliminate blockages. Its goal is to improve health by harmonizing these energy fields. According to research, it may help decrease pain and anxiety, enhance your mood and feeling of well-being, and aid in the treatment of depression.

What Does a Reiki Session Entail?

Reiki practitioners will put their hands on different areas of their or the other person's body to transmit healing energy. Practitioners may direct their energy during a session on the origins of particular problems. A normal Reiki session entails 20-90 minutes of meditative relaxation. All that is required is to shut one's eyes and surrender to the experience. Some people do fall asleep during sessions, which is OK. While working with the energy, the practitioner may listen to calming music.

Reiki sessions will most likely be given in a quiet, private environment by practitioners. It can, however, be performed anywhere. During a session, we will be fully dressed and sit in a comfy chair or on the ground.

After that, the practitioner will gently put their hands on or over particular regions of the head, limbs, and torso. They usually hold their hands in these positions for 3–10 minutes.

If the practitioner is treating a specific ailment—such as a burn—they will place their hands directly over the area.

According to believers, an energy transfer occurs when the practitioner gently places their hands on or over the body. During this period, the practitioner's hands may feel warm or tingly. As something releases, the individual (on whom Reiki is administered) feels warmth, tingling, or an ache. Some individuals claim to have seen visualizations—such as colors or images—or to have memories emerge. They may feel nothing at all at times. Each hand position will be held until the practitioner feels the energy has ceased flowing.

When the practitioner believes that the heat or energy in their hands has dissipated, they will withdraw their hands and put them over another body region.

Some Reiki practitioners may additionally concentrate on the chakras to ensure that energy is flowing freely without any blocks. They may use a crystal pendulum to check for movement by holding it over each chakra.

Reiki, according to practitioners, harnesses universal energy known as Ki, which is pronounced "Chi." This is the same energy that is used in Tai Chi. This energy is said to pervade the body. Reiki practitioners point out that, although this energy cannot be measured using current scientific methods, many people who tune in to it can feel it.

Reiki is said to help with relaxation, the body's natural healing processes, and the development of emotional, mental, and spiritual well-being.

Anecdotal data indicates it may produce profound relaxation, assist individuals in coping with challenges, alleviate emotional tension, and enhance general well-being.

Reiki has been used to treat the following conditions:

- Cancer
- Cardiovascular disease
- Anxiety
- Depression
- Long-term pain
- Infertility
- Neurodegenerative conditions

- Autism
- Crohn's disease
- Fatigue

It is crucial to note that Reiki should never be used instead of medical therapy.

People with specific health problems, on the other hand, may be interested in incorporating Reiki into their normal treatment regimen. Reiki, for example, may be helpful to certain cancer patients because it may help them relax. Reiki treatment's gentle nature may be calming to patients who are feeling overwhelmed by intrusive therapy, fear, and worry.

Individuals report varying levels of satisfaction. Some claim that the practitioner's hands grow heated, while others experience cooling hands and pulsing waves. The most frequent testimonials are of stress relief and profound relaxation.

And, although it may seem to be a gifted trait, anybody can perform Reiki, and it is simple to learn for anyone interested. The first level of study begins with understanding the history of Reiki, fundamental hand postures, and the nature of sensing energy. During the second level, students study symbols, particularly those for distance healing. The third level assists novice Reiki practitioners in understanding and mastering their own energy, while the fourth level qualifies trainees as Reiki "Masters."

Using this guide as a launchpad, I'll assist you in taking your Reiki practice from basic to simply out-of-this-world. You'll be able to use your newfound knowledge to assist yourself, friends, and family.

This book is a complete reference for Reiki students, practitioners, and masters alike. Through this I want you to learn about Reiki, a universal energy that has been utilized effectively to treat emotional, physical, and energetic imbalances all around the globe.

Whether you're new to Reiki or an experienced practitioner looking to expand your knowledge and skills, this guide will teach you how to use Reiki to heal yourself and others, eliminate energy blocks and cleanse the aura, cultivate and trust your natural intuition, and ground and protect yourself as a Reiki practitioner.

It will provide you with comprehensive help as you learn how to practice Reiki on yourself and others while studying specific knowledge from Reiki Levels I, II, and Master. This book will be useful for those who want to learn more about Reiki before enrolling in a formal program. It may also be used as a guidebook in Reiki training. Those wishing to review their understanding from their Reiki courses will also find this manual helpful. This book will be a reliable companion on your wonderful Reiki journey.

BASICS, HISTORY, AND PRINCIPLES OF REIKI

Reiki is the Japanese word for "Universal Life Force Energy," which is the life-giving energy that everyone has. To comprehend Reiki, think of it as our "experienced awareness of being alive." Reiki is a gentle touch therapy that includes the practitioner's hands being placed on different parts of the body to induce relaxation and a feeling of peace via energy transfer.

It is:

Intelligent: The energy is aware of where it should go and what it should do to assist you.

Natural: Other than the Reiki practitioner, who conducts Reiki energy via his hands, no other tools or gear is required.

Gentle: The practitioner gently puts their hands on or just above the body. Massage or manipulation are not used.

Simple to Comprehend: Reiki may be learned in three levels—1st degree, 2nd degree, and 3rd degree (Master level).

- **1st Level:** It is also known as Reiki I or Shoden in Japanese. It is introductory Reiki training in which you study Reiki history, learn how to conduct self-Reiki and how to provide Reiki to others, and are initiated (attuned) to the Reiki energy for life.
- **2nd Level:** Reiki II, or Okuden in Japanese, is the 2nd level. You will learn how to use the first 3 Reiki symbols as well as remote Reiki methods. You are given more

Reiki energy attunements. After completing this level, you will be considered a Reiki practitioner.
- **3rd Level (Master):** Reiki III, also known as Shinpiden in Japanese, is the 3rd level. This is the Master level of Reiki, and the lesson is divided into 2 halves. You are attuned to Master Reiki and learn the Master Reiki symbols as well as how to administer Reiki attunements to others.

Lifelong: Once you have been attuned to the Reiki, you will be able to channel Reiki for the rest of your life.

All Faiths or Belief Systems are Compatible: You can receive or practice Reiki regardless of your faith. Reiki is a relaxing and healing technique used by people of all religions.

Reiki Healing System Components

Reiki is made up of 5 main components that the practitioner utilizes to channel Reiki energy and cure himself and others. When prepared to offer or receive Reiki, go through the following checklist:

- **Hand Postures:** To determine where to put your hands during a Reiki session, use a series of positions.
- **Reiki Hand Postures for Self-Treatment:** Use these postures to treat yourself with Reiki.
- **Hand Postures for Treating Others:** Use these postures to treat others with Reiki.
- **Connecting to the Source:** Connect with the source of Reiki's global energy and concentrate the healing energy inside yourself via meditation and focusing.
- **Symbols:** To connect with Reiki energy, use the Reiki symbols and the sound of their names as a mantra.
- **Reiki Principles:** The 5 Reiki principles form the foundation of a regular meditation practice (We'll discuss Reiki principles ahead).

Reiki processes are known by names such as:
- Centering
- Clearing
- Beaming
- Getting rid of toxic energies
- Infusing
- Aura smoothing and raking

Some Reiki practitioners may also use crystals and chakra healing wands to facilitate healing and shield a home from bad energy.

While all this may seem like voodoo magic, even nonbelievers who have spent an hour with a competent Reiki master (as they're known) have felt a pleasant change of some kind. Many people describe Reiki treatments as soothing or centering. Reiki sessions are a mix of gentle touch and above-the-body energy sweeping. For others, it's more of an emotional readjustment.

But how did Reiki become popular? Where did it come from, and what is its origin?

The History

Reiki's origins may be traced back to ancient Chinese and Japanese medicine. It is based on Qi ("Chi"), which practitioners describe as universal life energy.

Although there are numerous types of energy therapy in civilizations throughout the globe, Dr. Mikao Usui, a Buddhist monk turned Japanese doctor, created Reiki in the late 1800s. He found the power to heal via soft touch or close contact while meditating for 21 days (However, people have been practicing Reiki for over 2,500 years).

Usui was a lay monk with a wife and two children who had been a spiritual seeker his whole life. Various lineages of Buddhist, Taoist, and Shinto practices coexisted as major elements in Japanese spirituality and culture throughout Usui's time.

Usui's rigorous spiritual efforts resulted in a profound epiphany, which gave rise to the technique now known as Reiki. This insight was most likely made around 1922.

During the final four years of his life, Usui traveled extensively throughout Japan, imparting his spiritual teachings to almost 2,000 young disciples but only training 16 as Reiki masters. Chujiro Hayashi, one of his master disciples, was a former navy officer. Hayashi collaborated with Usui to extract therapeutic techniques from Usui's broader body of teachings for them to be more broadly disseminated. He was the one who diversified the practice, incorporating many of the hand postures that are still in use today.

Hayashi established a Reiki clinic in Tokyo with Usui's approval, where 16 practitioners worked in pairs to provide therapy. Hawayo Takata, a first-generation Japanese-American, sought treatment at Hayashi's clinic for a variety of medical problems, including asthma. Takata's health was recovered after months of therapy, and she became a dedicated student.

Takata introduced Reiki to Hawaii in 1937, and then to the US mainland, with Hayashi's active supervision and support. Takata had been practicing and teaching Reiki for 40 years before educating Reiki masters. His teachings have been passed down via 22 Reiki masters since her death in December 1980. Thus, Reiki has grown in popularity and is now practiced all around the globe, though not always in the original manner Takata taught.

Reiki therapy has been utilized more often in hospital settings since the early 1990s. It is extensively used in healthcare as an adjunct to, never as a replacement for, patients' normal medical therapy and medicines. This is due to Reiki's ability to facilitate the body's inherent healing powers.

Reiki is used as a supplementary treatment in over 900 institutions and healthcare systems in the United States. It was non-hazardous to patients in any way, and it is safe to use Reiki with chemotherapy, radiation, and medicines used in cancer treatment.

Reiki Principles

Reiki, like other spiritual practices, is founded on a set of principles. These basic premises are akin to affirmations or goals. They provide advice for connecting with your Reiki energy by concentrating on the present moment, which may assist improve your feeling of well-being in a variety of ways. They guide you through the process of healing and balancing your Reiki energy.

Reiki practitioners adhere to the 5 principles of Reiki as spiritual guidelines. They promote Reiki's spiritual goals and serve as the foundation for a practitioner's lifestyle. The 5 principles were translated from Japanese, and although certain translations may differ significantly, the principles' meaning remains consistent.

Today's translation of the 5 Reiki Principles is as follows:

1. Just for Today, I Release Angry Thoughts
2. Just for Today, I Release Thoughts of Worry
3. Just for Today, I'm Grateful
4. Just for Today, I Expand My Consciousness
5. Just for Today, I'm Gentle with All Beings

Each of the 5 principles begins with the phrase "Just for today," as a reminder that when life seems stressful, we may concentrate on how we respond to it one day at a time. The 5 principles should not be used as self-judgment rules, but rather as a reminder of what we aspire towards. If you cannot meet them, it is totally fine since you may wipe the slate clean and begin over tomorrow.

Let's go through these Reiki principles and how you may use them to assist you to generate more positivity in your daily life.

1. Just for Today, I Release Angry Thoughts

It's natural to get furious from time to time. Anger is a deep-seated emotion that is destructive and dangerous. Its manifestation causes pain and yields nothing. Regardless, it is a feeling that we all feel and experience. Fear or restrictive beliefs often motivate it. This feeling may be provoked by a variety of situations—such as dealing with a nasty co-worker or being cut off in traffic.

However, according to Reiki, anger is not caused by external circumstances. Instead, it is caused by the furious energy that already exists inside you.

This concept is intended to assist you in releasing this energy. It helps you to identify and let go of your anger, enabling you to welcome happiness into your life.

The goal is not to feel angry but to recognize it when it emerges, understand the causes, and avoid reacting to it. Surrender your wrath to the Universal Source and it will eradicate its destructive character. If you feed into it, it will drag you down.

By saying aloud, "Just for Today, I Release Angry Thoughts," you are making a deliberate decision that anger will not rule your day, emotions, or actions. It is letting anger glide through like a wind with no connection. It loses its strength and grip on you when you do this.

2. Just for Today, I Release Thoughts of Worry

Worry is a low-vibrational emotion based on the dread of "what if" situations. We are nervous and terrified because we are preoccupied with unpleasant potential events. While it's natural to believe that concern originates from the outside, Reiki believes it begins inside.

Thinking about future occurrences may rise unpleasant feelings if you are hanging on to worry energy. However, if you can let go of this energy, you may find it easier to live in the present moment and worry less about the future.

By mentally and vocally saying, "Just for Today, I Release Thoughts of Worry," you are asking your higher power to relieve you of the tension and concern of tomorrow. You are bringing yourself back to the present moment and believing that whatever happens will be in your best interests. Letting go of tomorrow might be the most difficult thing to accomplish, but keep practicing and growing your trust. One day, you will be worry-free and your life and health will improve greatly as a result.

3. Just for Today, I'm Grateful

This is a reminder to be thankful for all you have. Practicing gratitude increases our general well-being, makes us happy, and fortifies our emotions by keeping destructive sentiments at bay. Slowing down and appreciating the wonderful in your life may assist you in cultivating more positive energy.

When we concentrate on the good aspects of our lives, we learn they are more rewarding than we previously imagined. We educate ourselves to appreciate what we have by saying, "Just for Today, I'm Grateful." Our lives become healthier, happier, and more plentiful as a result.

4. Just for Today, I Expand My Consciousness

Actively exercising awareness is essential in Reiki for balancing your energy. This concept invites you to reflect on how you've become more aware of the importance of enjoying the present moment.

5. Just for Today, I'm Gentle with All Beings

This principle emphasizes how being nice to others allows you to get good energy in return. It entails being kind with oneself, which is necessary for spiritual wellness.

People, animals, plants, the environment, and all its inhabitants contribute to our collective energy. "Just for today, I will be nice to my neighbor and all living creatures," encourages us to be kind and compassionate to others no matter how different our points of view, our financial situation, or our job title is. We acknowledge the critical role we all play in our collective progress by recognizing and showing compassion to one another. We must also be kind to ourselves since many of us are our harshest critics. The kinder you are to others and to yourself, the more compassion you will get.

How Can You Use Reiki Principles in Your Everyday Life?

Reiki principles may be used as mantras to help direct our thoughts and actions throughout the day. Reiki practitioners believe that this promotes spiritual and personal growth, allowing one to live a happier, more satisfying, and balanced life.

Here's how to use these principles as everyday mantras or guides.

1. Recognize and Let Go of Anger

"I release angry thoughts," the 1st principle focuses on changing your relationship with anger.

To use this concept in your life, do the following steps:

- Say aloud or to yourself, "Just for today, I release angry thoughts."
- Consider a time when you were furious today. Think of any rage you had the day before if you just woke up.
- Consider previous occurrences that are similar to current occurrences. Evaluate your feelings.
- Request assistance from your higher self in releasing

these furious thoughts and emotions.
- Take multiple slow, deep breaths. Consider releasing angry energy with each exhalation.

2. Recognize and Let Go of Worries

You may also embody the 2nd principle, "I release worrying thoughts," by releasing worried thoughts deliberately.

Here's how it works:

- Say loudly or to yourself, "Just for today, I release thoughts of worry."
- Consider a time when you were concerned today. Think about the times you worried yesterday if you simply woke up.
- Consider comparable situations from your past. Look for parallels between your previous and present feelings.
- Ask your higher self to assist you in letting go of your concerns.
- Take a few slow, deep breaths. Consider expelling worrying energy with each exhalation.

3. Exercise Gratitude

"I'm grateful," the 3rd principle, entails the act of being appreciative.

To show appreciation consciously:

- Say loudly or to yourself, "Just for today, I'm grateful."
- Consider every good person, item, and situation in your life. Take a moment to thank each of them.
- Allow each thought to fill your heart to overflowing.

4. Recognize Your Consciousness

The 4th principle, "I extend my consciousness," entails being aware of your own awareness. Mindfulness is about paying attention to the present moment and living in it.

Begin by repeating the principle to yourself or aloud. Next, imagine a time when you have lately experienced increased awareness, such as:

- Being present in the moment
- Feeling grateful
- Practicing some kind of meditation
- Going for a stroll in meditation

5. Feel Empathy towards Others

The 5th principle entails admitting when you've been cruel. This enables you to recognize how you feel and then let go of those feelings.

Here's how it works:

- Say aloud or to yourself, "Just for today, I'm kind with all creatures, including myself."
- Consider how you have been cruel to yourself or others today.
- Recognize any feelings of guilt or fear associated with these occurrences. Request your higher self to release that energy.
- Take a few slow, deep breaths. Consider expelling that bad energy with each exhalation.

REIKI'S FOUNDATIONAL PILLARS

Reiki practice is divided into 3 main components or pillars. Meditation, Spiritual and Energetic Development, and Hands-on Healing. These 3 pillars of Reiki assist Reiki practitioners in learning to interpret body energies and creating a respectful pattern of Shamanic communication. These pillars may seem straightforward, yet they are extremely sacred and, as such, set the tone for the Reiki session.

The following are the goals of these pillars:

- Acting as a source of spiritual hygiene by putting the Reiki practitioner in a peaceful and concentrated state of mind before and throughout Reiki channeling.
- Allowing the practitioner's ego to stand aside so that intuitive knowledge from Reiki energy, their healing partner, and Divine guidance may be received.
- Associating the practitioner and his healing partner with Reiki energy
- Enabling the practitioner to operate more instinctively while channeling Reiki energy to their healing partner.
- Creating an "envelope" of awareness for the practitioner during the session.

The 1st Pillar: Meditation (Gassho)

Meditation is the 1st pillar of Reiki. All other work is built based on meditation. Meditation brings our body, mind, and soul into harmony. Numerous studies have been conducted to demonstrate the effects of meditation on general health and mood.

"Anapanasati," or mindful practice, is the basic meditation used in Reiki. The technique used to develop mindful practice is Gassho.

Gassho roughly translates to "two hands joining." It is a ceremonial gesture produced by putting the hands—palms together, in the 'prayer' or 'praying hands' posture, and is the most basic and also the most often used of all the hand gestures (also known as in-zou and mudras) in Buddhist practice. It is a simple and efficient way to relax the mind and increase our vitality.

Meaning: Gassho means to bring two hands together

Pronunciation: Gassho pronounced Gash-sho

Buddhism: Mudra of Heart Work

Sanskrit: Anjali Mudra

Gassho meditation prepares us for Reiki and lays the groundwork for self-healing. It is used to awaken the Reiki energy within. In it, we join hands in prayer as a symbol of the divine unity of Father and Mother or God and Goddess. It is conducted as part of a Reiki practitioner's daily routine, lasting 15-30 minutes, ideally in the morning or evening.

The left hand in this mudra symbolizes human people in the physical world, while the right hand represents the Buddha, an enlightened creature. The action of clasping hands shows that we, too, may become enlightened beings like the Buddha. The route to enlightenment is via inner stillness, which Gassho practice gets us closer to.

Allow yourself time to experience meditation if you have never done it before or are a novice. During meditation, a restless mind might make us feel uncomfortable and unpleasant. If this is occurring to you, begin with a few minutes of meditation and gradually increase your time as you improve. You will notice how quiet you will feel with time, and your mental restlessness will lessen.

The Steps:

It's a very long and precise process, we'll discuss it in detail later in the book. This is just an overview of the practice.

1. Place yourself in a peaceful area where you will not be bothered or distracted. You may sit on a chair, on a meditation cushion, or on the floor in the easy pose (cross-legged).
2. Straighten the spine, shut your eyes, and put your hands together in prayer posture. The hands should be placed in front of the heart.
3. It is a good idea to have a focus point throughout this meditation to keep the mind quiet. You may concentrate on your breathing, the feeling of your hands touching, or the spot where your two middle fingers connect.
4. Visualize the Reiki energy entering you through the Crown to the Root Chakra, energizing each chakra.
5. Bring your focus back to your body, to your hands and feet, to finish this meditation. Take a few deep breaths and open your eyes.

Some practitioners find it beneficial to listen to soothing music while meditating, while others prefer quiet. Do what seems natural to you (I suggest avoiding music). Setting an intention before beginning, repeating a mantra, or reciting the 5 Reiki principles may all be done as part of your Gassho meditation. This should not seem like an extra task for you to do. You are giving yourself a gift that will bring more serenity, pleasure, and love into your life.

Gassho meditation is a crucial practice in Reiki and the life of a healer. This meditation has no purpose. You are merely to become present in your body and feel the calmness inside you. Allow thoughts to come and go as they please, without attachment or judgment. Gassho meditation heightens our consciousness and provides us the quiet required to connect with our higher selves, the intuitive aspect of ourselves that will lead our hands in a Reiki healing session and in life.

It also acts as a type of spiritual hygiene, a ritual for creating intention and concentration, an invitation to mindfulness, a call to leave aside ego, and the primary means for inviting and activating Reiki healing energy in a session.

The 2nd Pillar: Spiritual and Energetic Development (Reiji-Ho)

Gassho is integrated with the other 2 pillars of Reiki. The 2nd pillar, Reiji-Ho, is about seeking direction. Reiji is a Japanese word that means "indication of Reiki force." Ho translates as "methods." Reiji-Ho is made up of 3 brief rituals that may be done before each Reiki session.

While 1st degree Reiki practitioners learn the Reiki hand positions, they may eventually feel comfortable enough to work instinctively. Reiki students are urged to work intuitively as much as possible during Reiki sessions, understanding that they can always revert to the hand positions if necessary.

Spiritual Development is the 2nd pillar of Reiki. Spiritual growth is taught at all Reiki levels. Consider meditation to be the stretching and warmup we do before we exercise. We conduct aerobics and resistance training for spiritual growth. We strengthen our "energetic" muscles so that we can perform tasks more simply and effectively.

It is taking a minute to recognize that the Source has responded to the request to open the energy channel and make the energy connections. This pillar allows you to convey thoughts and prayers of gratitude for the newly created energy path.

You also welcome guidance in Reiji-ho. It starts in Gassho, with your hands held in prayer posture, requesting to be directed to serve the highest and greatest benefit of your healing to anyone with your hands and energies. Then you wait and listen with all your senses. Pay attention to how your body feels, what your mind is thinking, what your eyes perceive, and how your healing partner reacts (if any). Wait for direction by observing with all your senses and allowing your mind to empty so that it may become a vessel into which guidance can readily flow.

You will gradually come to understand how the Divine guidance communicates with you. You could notice a twitch and sense something in your body. In your mind, you may hear instructions. You may feel magnetically pulled to a certain portion of the body that needs healing. There is no correct or incorrect method to receive information.

Reiji-Ho requires faith in oneself, one's healing partner, one's Divine guidance system, Reiki, and the cosmos. It also requires mindfulness. You must be energetically open to become a vessel used by the cosmos to serve the highest and largest benefit. When you get a signal, believe it, act on it, and trust that Reiki energy will flow precisely where and when it is required for the highest and greatest benefit. Return to Gassho and re-set yourself when you sense yourself drifting out of that place as a vessel.

The Steps:
- Raise your hands in front of your heart in the Gassho pose. With your eyes closed, request the Reiki energy to flow through you.
- Inquire about the recipient's recovery and well-being. Raise your hands to your Third Eye and ask to be directed to the location where Reiki energy is required.
- Allow your hands to lead you. Detach from any expect-

ations you may have for the session's result and center your focus on the Reiki energy and your intuition.

The 3rd Pillar: Hands-on Healing (Chiryo)

Once the first 2 pillars are in place, the practitioner can perform hands-on healing. This is another Shamanic thread that allows the receiver to comprehend the process that is unfolding, to learn to speak more clearly and directly with his body and to comprehend how profoundly and quickly the Source and Spirit Guide energy comes to his help. The Reiki practitioner must stay open and clear to distinguish the body's signals as well as communications from the Source.

Chiryo is the Japanese term for "treatment" which is hands-on healing. It's all about taking action. It is the therapy in and of itself. Reiki energy is passed via the practitioner's hands and into the recipient. Breath connects the body and awareness. We inhale oxygen for bodily survival and the universal life energy to nourish and cleanse our spirits.

Chiryo involves the mechanical process of putting the dominant hands on the body in certain locations and believing that the Reiki will flow where it is required. However, when a practitioner gets more deeply immersed in the actual practice of Reiki, Chiryo flows and changes based on intuitive knowledge received by the Reiki practitioner and the requirements of healing. The Reiki practitioner continues to apply their intuition when it comes to hand placement until the session is brought to a conclusion.

A practitioner who is genuinely involved in Chiryo goes beyond the fundamental hand postures and, in certain cases, even beyond the use of the hands. He or she may be prompted instinctively to look, tap, stroke, blow, or envision, as well as to place hands, palms, or fingers in the ways that they are guided to do so. A conscious Reiki session becomes a fluid dance of energy that encompasses the practitioner, his or her healing partner, and the whole cosmos in this manner.

REIKI ADVANTAGES

Today's fast-paced lifestyle may cause stress, which can disrupt your mental, emotional, and physical balance, leading to illness. As a result, it is essential to develop a daily routine that will allow you to release stress and relax, resulting in happiness and inner peace. Reiki is one example of an alternative practice. This spiritually based life force healing not only improves one's health but also one's quality of life. Daily Reiki practice may help your body reach mental, spiritual, and physical equilibrium.

This energy healing approach has become a huge sensation; wellness practitioners and health experts alike have all gushed about the advantages of Reiki, and even celebrities have embraced this alternative treatment method.

Gentle touch, optimistic thinking, and energy transfer have all been shown to generate dramatic outcomes. It is gentle, soothing, and non-traumatic, and it may be readily included in any comprehensive health and lifestyle plan. Reiki therapy is a deep and powerful way for healing on a multi-layered and comprehensive level—mind, body, and spirit—whether you are searching for emotional trauma recovery, energy level balance, or spiritual development.

Here are just a few of the many benefits of Reiki:

1. Aids in the Alleviation of Stress

Reiki's most well-documented health advantages include stress reduction and relaxation. This Japanese energy healing method, in fact, is intended to activate your body's relaxation response and relieve tension.

Most diseases nowadays are connected to stress in some way, whether it be environmental stress, occupational stress, or emotional stress. In fact, these elements account for most of the therapy's health advantages.

- Stress may cause abnormal heart rhythms, which can lead to angina or stroke.
- Because common hormones such as leptin and ghrelin affect the brain and stomach, stress causes gastrointestinal disorders.
- Eating disorders are a typical result of stress since when you are anxious, you tend to overeat or have an aversion to eating.
- Stress causes mood disorders and a variety of psychiatric issues.
- Male sexual issues might be exacerbated by stress.

Reiki's biofield energy healing approach is intended to stimulate the body's relaxation response, enhance positive energy, and decrease stress, all of which help the immune system battle sickness. The biofield is the scientific name for the delicate vibrating energy field that surrounds and links our physical bodies.

Reiki improved the symptoms of sadness and stress in a one-year trial of 45 individuals. Even after a year of therapy, the positive benefits persisted.

2. Relieves Inflammation and Infections

Many diseases may be caused by stress. Reiki not only relieves stress but also boosts the immune system's ability to fight illnesses. Because of its stress-relieving properties, it may strengthen the immune system, allowing it to more effectively repair and minimize infections and inflammation in the body.

This may seem like a miracle, but according to one fascinating discovery published in the journal Alternative and Complementary Medicine, Reiki resulted in speedier inflammation and infection recovery. Hepatitis C was cured in an obese hypertensive patient. Anemia and neutropenia were negative effects of the medication (severe deficiency of neutrophils, a type of white blood cell, leading to susceptibility to infection). Reiki treatment was given to him to alleviate his anxiety and improve his overall well-being. In addition, the physicians saw that his neutrophil count and hematocrit had greatly increased, which enhanced bone marrow function. So much so that even after a year of therapy, the patient remained infection-free.

3. It Eases Depression and Anxiety

Reiki has been examined for its capacity to relieve anxiety in both healthy participants and medical patients.

Anxiety and depression are strongly linked to mood changes. A lot of studies have shown that Reiki has general mood improvements. The advantages are confined to those who are in a bad mood.

According to the research, when your mood increases, it is accompanied by less anxiety. Not only will your anxiety lessen, but you will also notice a big drop in depression, rage, and confusion. Your positive energy grows, as does the lack of enthusiasm that occurs with depression.

In a brief study published in 2010, researchers investigated the effects of Reiki on elderly persons suffering from pain, despair, or anxiety. Participants reported improvements in their health symptoms, happiness, and overall well-being. They also reported greater sensations of calm, increased curiosity, and improved self-care.

4. Improves Mobility for Shoulder, Wrist, or Lower Back Discomfort

An intriguing research published in the Complementary and Alternative Medicine Journal compared the efficacy of an increasing range of motion via physical therapy and Reiki and discovered that both had the same impact on improving the range of motion (ROM) of the afflicted area.

These findings imply that the positive effects of Reiki and ROM may be due to changes in local joint or muscle structures, rather than the pain system.

5. Improves Metabolic Syndrome Indices

Metabolic syndrome—a collection of symptoms linked to an increased risk of type 2 diabetes, heart disease, and other chronic illnesses—affects a large and growing proportion of the global population. Physical exercise is arguably the most effective way to improve metabolic syndrome outcomes, although Reiki has also been shown to be useful.

Many people, particularly those who are overweight and sedentary and are at high risk of developing metabolic syndrome, may be unable or reluctant to engage in traditional kinds of physical activity such as strength training and gym-based activities. According to Joel Anderson and Ann Gill Taylor at the Center for the Study of Complementary and Alternative Therapies, University of Virginia School of Nursing, Charlottesville, USA, "mind-body modalities are simple, inexpensive, noninvasive therapies that are easy to learn and can be practiced easily by individuals who may experience potential mobility limitations."

Although the researchers did not expressly name Reiki, they did endorse the potential therapeutic usefulness of mind-body treatments as supportive care modalities for metabolic syndrome management, particularly insulin resistance and high blood pressure.

6. Allows for Emotional Clarity

Reiki not only cures you physically but also heals you emotionally. One of the most attractive benefits of Reiki is that it may improve your capacity to love and empathize by allowing you to connect closely with others. That's why Reiki is rapidly gaining a recognized presence in hospitals and clinics, maybe due to the therapeutic approach's non-traumatic nature and ease of integration with conventional therapy.

It has the potential to improve your relationships. It has the potential to mend your personal relationships. Reiki promotes inner calm and harmony, which are necessary for spiritual progress. It's a 'cleaner' and a "clearer" for your emotions.

7. Improves Memory and Behaviour

Reiki sessions improved behavior and memory issues in a research including 24 individuals with moderate cognitive impairment or mild Alzheimer's disease when compared to the control group.

8. Encourages Healing and Growth

An exploratory cell study found that Reiki greatly increased the growth of heat-shocked bacterial colonies. The authors speculate that this might reflect the ability of Reiki to aid in the healing of injuries in both animals and humans, though this interpretation is a bit of a stretch and has not been supported by other research.

9. Alleviates Pain and Fatigue

A study of randomized trials found that Reiki may help to alleviate pain and discomfort. It may also aid in the reduction of fatigue.

A 2015 research discovered that persons receiving cancer treatment who also got remote Reiki had decreased levels of pain, anxiety, and exhaustion. These levels were much lower than those seen in the control group, which simply received medical attention. For 5 days, participants received 30-minute sessions of remote Reiki.

Another 2015 study looked at the impact of Reiki on women after cesarean delivery. They discovered that Reiki dramatically lowered pain, anxiety, and the pace of breathing in women 1-2 days following a cesarean birth. The number and demand for analgesic pain relievers were also decreased. Reiki had no impact on either blood pressure or pulse rate.

In a 2018 study, researchers compared the use of Reiki to physiotherapy for alleviating lower back pain in persons with herniated discs. Both therapies were equally efficient in relieving pain, however, Reiki was more cost-effective and led to faster healing in some cases.

10. Improves One's Quality of Life

Reiki's pleasant effects may improve your overall well-being. It shows considerable gains in the physical, environmental, and social elements of quality of life in general.

In a tiny 2016 study, researchers discovered that Reiki was beneficial in increasing the quality of life for cancer patients. Women who received Reiki saw changes in their sleep habits, self-esteem, and depression levels. They reported feelings of serenity, inner peace, and relaxation.

11. Improves Mood

Reiki may help you feel better by alleviating worry and despair. According to the findings of a 2011 research, persons who received Reiki saw better mood benefits than those who did not get Reiki. Participants in the research who received six 30-minute sessions spread out over 2-8 weeks exhibited improvements in their mood.

12. Promotes Stability and Harmony

Reiki is a non-invasive energy transfer technique that is exceptionally successful in boosting general well-being. It may be a powerful technique for restoring your body's balance on all levels—including mental, emotional, and physical—so that all body components work in perfect harmony. The body can restore equilibrium across all systems via energy transmission. This promotes unity and helps individuals to maintain a happy way of life.

When a body works in harmony, it enhances its inherent healing capacities, which improves overall health and wellness. Reiki for infants may be particularly beneficial in this area. It may aid in the development and expansion of the baby's hearing.

13. Aids in Relaxation

The relaxation reaction, which practitioners claim activates the body's natural healing mechanism, is at the heart of the most well-documented upsides of Reiki.

It may be a really quiet and pleasant experience that leaves you feeling revived. Stressed people might try Reiki for anxiety, since it may motivate them to release all of their tension, stress, and bad sentiments to achieve a condition of serenity, health, and well-being.

14. Helps One Sleep Better

Reiki improves sleep by stimulating the body to attain its natural balance and inner healing. When your mind is at ease and devoid of anxieties and concerns, you are more likely to sleep soundly. The more calm a person is, the more productive and busy they may be without being fatigued, stressed, or burned out.

After a Reiki session, you always feel very calm. This kind of relaxation aids our bodies' ability to sleep better, recover faster, and think more clearly. During a Reiki session, it is not unusual for individuals to fall asleep.

A 2012 research examined 40 women suffering from anxiety and insomnia. For 10 weeks, half of the group got Reiki treatments twice a week, while the other half received no therapy. The ladies who got Reiki had substantial improvements in their depressive symptoms as well as their sleep quality.

15. Treats Cancer-Related Symptoms

Reiki, or any other mind-body treatment for that matter, cannot heal cancer. However, they may successfully cure cancer-related symptoms—such as sadness, pain, and fatigue. Reiki for cancer patients might be one technique to assist them to cope with the exhaustion and discomfort that most cancer therapies cause. It may be used to psychologically prepare individuals to battle cancer, therefore enhancing their quality of life. Similarly, Reiki reduces migraine, sciatica, and arthritic pain. It also aids in the treatment of asthma, menopause, and insomnia.

For example, in a study published in the journal Integrative Cancer Therapy, researchers reported that treating cancer patients with Reiki for 5 consecutive days, followed by a 1-week break, then 2 additional Reiki sessions, could significantly reduce tiredness, pain, and anxiety, as well as improve quality of life.

In a study of 100 cancer patients, the benefits of Reiki vs placebo ("sham" or faux Reiki) were examined. The group that got "real" Reiki therapy had a much greater quality of life, indicating a genuine effect.

16. Personal Relationships are Improved

Reiki may help you heal and progress in your personal relationships by emotionally rebuilding you. It may improve your capacity to relate to and connect with others on a deeper level, hence improving your relationships. It may cleanse your aura of negative energies, allowing you to experience inner peace and, as a result, improve your capacity to love and open up to others, allowing relationships to develop. You could start responding to life situations and people in a more helpful, trusting manner rather than negative.

17. Reduces Pain Perception

Reiki may aid in the reduction of pain perception by mending the emotional side of pain. Reiki is intended to alleviate emotional discomfort by enabling healing energy to flow freely throughout the body, resulting in relaxation and decreased pain and tension throughout the body. It may also help reduce tension and anxiety, which can lead to a reduction in pain perception.

Reiki was shown to be equally beneficial as physical therapy in increasing the range of motion in individuals with painful shoulder limitations in a pilot research with 78 participants.

Another pilot research found that 16% of patients who got Reiki together with a sedative drug before colonoscopy required less pain medication during the operation than the control group.

18. Reflects Our Inner Self

Many individuals like Reiki because it enables them to just "be." It is a few minutes of pure relaxation during which the recipient may clear their minds and relieve the strain and stress of the day. Reiki energy transfer may help individuals feel tranquil, relaxed, and lighter, allowing them to connect with their inner selves and reflect clearly on their life.

19. Breaks Down Energy Blocks

Reiki treatment raises one's consciousness, allowing them to become more aware of the issues that seem to deprive them of their serenity and pleasure. It may aid in the removal of energy obstacles—such as negative thoughts or self-deprecating sentiments—to bring about tranquility. One learns to listen to their body and mind to make appropriate, mindful choices for their health. Being conscious of your own needs may help you get access to inner wisdom and understanding, which can help you cope with daily stress more effectively.

This reduces stress, improves learning and memory, increases mental clarity, and promotes physical healing/less physical discomfort. When energy pathways are obstructed, good energy cannot reach certain portions of the body, resulting in mood swings, anxiety, rage, pain, and other symptoms. Reiki may help keep these pathways clean.

20. Toxins are Removed from the Body, and the Immune system is Strengthened

The Reiki method is used to remind our bodies of how to return to a state of "repair" or "self-healing" rest and digest. By inducing this condition, our bodies begin to purge themselves of unwanted energy. It also enables the body to defend itself against weariness, burnout, and immune system failure.

Regular Reiki sessions can help your body cleanse itself of dangerous toxins, thus strengthening your immune system. Most individuals are always in a stress-response battle mode, which disrupts their body's natural balance and immunity, making them more prone to illness. Their bodies, in fact, forget how to re-establish the equilibrium. Reiki may play a vital part in reminding the body to transition into a rest/digest self-healing mode, which may aid in the body's natural defense mechanisms being strengthened.

21. Centers Us to the Present Moment

Reiki urges its users to live in the present moment. It may help you be aware of the present moment by letting go of past regrets and future worries. The positive energy transfer permits the mind to focus on present events rather than dwelling on previous errors or worrying about the future. This will aid in accepting how life unfolds and will encourage good responses to events, people, and circumstances.

It can heal emotional and mental traumas, alleviate anxiety and irritation, and improve mental clarity and learning. It may improve your capacity to manage or handle circumstances and events that do not always go as planned.

22. Increases the Body's Ability to Heal Itself

Reiki restores your internal body levels to a near-natural condition. As a result, your respiration, heart rate, blood pressure, circulation, and other body systems will improve. This typical state of equilibrium will enable your body to repair itself from the inside.

23. Strengthens Emotional Well-Being

Reiki—like mindfulness meditation—promotes emotional development and tranquility in practitioners and patients, resulting in enhanced mental clarity, capacity for love and empathy, and emotional well-being.

24. Cleanses the Aura

Do you get ill a lot too frequently and are always irritable and tense? Are you unable to sleep properly, and your body and mind seem to be in a constant state of weariness? If you relate to these indications and symptoms, it may be time to clean your aura.

The energy field that surrounds your body is termed your 'Aura.' It functions as an energetic magnetic field that catches up on emotions, health, psychic garbage, and the circumstances surrounding you. Your aura might be strained when you trade energy with individuals around you, which is why you should clean your auric field regularly. Reiki is particularly effective in clearing these bad energies from your aura.

25. Promotes Spiritual Growth

I can't emphasize enough that Reiki treats the whole person—mind, body, and soul. This shows that the positive energy transfer provided by Reiki is beneficial in improving the receiver's mood and overall perspective on life. The healing that begins inside will have an impact on their choices and outlook on the outside.

Reiki sessions propel a person's self-healing path via personal growth. It promotes the traits of understanding, love, and acceptance and aids in creating a connection with the soul. It teaches a person to accept himself as he is and to have compassion for others.

Reiki may be used to heal people in a variety of ways. Just one thing to note, Reiki does not target a specific issue inside the body but treats everything at once...

THE ENERGY ARCHITECTURE OF THE BODY

Look under the surface—the world that includes your clothing, skin, material belongings, and everything you can see—and you'll find a cosmos of whirling and delicate energies. These are the energies that underpin physical reality; they create you and all else you perceive.

The traditional Newtonian-physics-based vision of the body as a sophisticated machine is progressively losing way to a new scientific worldview of the body as a complex energy system. This worldview is founded on a new Einsteinian and quantum physics viewpoint that "the biological components that comprise the physical body are really a kind of vibrating energy."

To comprehend the Reiki energy system, we must first recognize that our body comprises more than only muscles, bones, nerves, and organs, but also of a subtle energy system through which life-force energy flows. The energy bodies communicate with one another through energy centers, which act as valves, enabling the life force to flow throughout the body.

If you look in the mirror, you will most likely see your physical body. You are aware of your skin, hair, and nails. You can see a face as well as some of your sense organs. You may observe your clothing, facial expression, physique, and the structure formed by what is under the surface—your muscles, bones, fat, and organs.

We are most familiar with our physical bodies because we experience them through our five senses. We devote a significant amount of effort to responding to our bodily demands because they can't be neglected. We must eat and sleep. We need to get moving and relax. We need to heal when we are ill. We want the pain to stop when we are in it. The demands of your physical body are urgent and pressing, and you are constantly aware of them. Your body is made up of several physical systems and organs—such as your neurological system, digestive system, circulatory system, and so on.

Your physical body also contains your brain, which is the physical manifestation of your intellect. Every day, you use your brain. It regulates a variety of physiological processes, both conscious and unconscious (thinking, speaking, walking, conversing, etc). (breathing, digestion, heartbeat, etc.).

Your brain (and nervous system) are also the parts of your body that enable you to experience bodily sensations such as pain or pleasure, as well as sensory input such as touch, taste, sight, smell, and noises. It is a component of your mind, but it is not the whole picture. Your awareness is a non-physical component of your mind. It is the part of yourself that perceives, feels, and dreams. It is the region in which the ego lives and where the concepts of separation and dualism take root. Your mind is responsible for your perception of your existence and experiences in three-dimensional space.

Finally, there is a totally non-physical component of you that you may refer to as your spirit or soul. This is the everlasting, higher portion of you. It is multidimensional and exists beyond the three-dimensional realm in which your body resides. Soul connects you to higher realms such as creation, source, God, and Divinity. The soul is in charge of inherent abilities—such as inspiration, intuition, creativity, love, compassion, kindness, and humility.

All these characteristics exist in you, and your energetic systems, or energy anatomy, link the three—body, mind, and spirit. Your energy systems serve as conduits between the physical and non-physical worlds. They are the reason we are still alive. They contain Ki/Chi, which flows through us. Ki travels around us in an energy field known as the aura, via our system's energy centers known as Chakras, and inside the physical body via routes known as Meridians. Thus, your energy system is divided into 3 parts: Aura, Meridians, and Chakras.

Let's take a closer look at each of them:

Aura

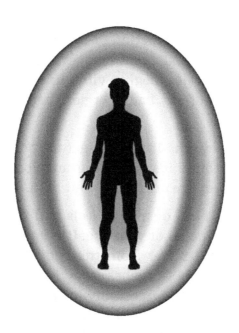

The cosmos is described as energy in quantum physics, with energy and matter interchangeable. Life is referred to as energy in psychology, Eastern treatment, and alternative medicine. The aura may be thought of as an energy field that surrounds the body and interacts with it on spiritual and psychological levels through structures known as Chakras. In other terms, the aura is an energy field that surrounds the physical body and may be seen by people with psychical vision.

Everything that is living—including trees, plants, animals, and humans—has an aura. The aura is your energy imprint that radiates from your body. Auras come in a variety of hues that vary continuously based on moods and emotions, diseases or health, and a plethora of other factors that influence your electromagnetic field. By exposing a photographic plate to a high electric field, Kirlian photographers may capture pictures of your aura.

Your aura has both protective and reactive properties. It responds to everything that influences your energy and also keeps energy near to you. Many people think that all disease starts in the aura and may last for many years before manifesting in the actual body. Any obstruction or imbalance in the aura's energy may lead to physical, emotional, or mental disease. Therefore, many energy healers begin a vibrational healing session by cleansing the aura of any bad energies that have gotten stuck there.

Tell me, have you ever had someone get too near to you and you didn't want to be there? It's unsettling, and you remark, "He/she is in my space." They are present in your aura.

Your aura is composed of many levels and planes that reflect various energy elements of your life. It is composed of 7 layers and often extends 2-3 feet from the body. Your Etheric Aura is closest to your body (2 inches away from the skin) and reflects what is going on energetically in your physical body. The Emotional Aura, which is a bit farther out, represents your emotional condition. Following that are lower and higher Mental Auras, each a bit farther away from the body. These represent your brain's thinking patterns as well as your mind's thought patterns. The Astral Aura comes next, and it represents your spiritual characteristics—such as your understandings, spiritual studies, and so on. The next layer contains information on your dreams and intuition. Finally, the Ketheric Aura plane, which is the farthest away from the body, is a balancing component of your aura that helps integrate all the other levels. This layer contains your whole spiritual blueprint. It contains your Akashic DNA. Your Akash (or Akashic record) is the portion of your everlasting soul that contains all of your experiences and understandings from the beginning of your life to the present.

As a result, when someone mentions an "Aura," they're referring to the invisible spiritual energy field that surrounds all living things. It functions as an energetic magnetic field, picking up on emotions, health, psychic trash, and the environment that surrounds you. Your aura may be stressed when you trade energy with people around you, which is why you should clean your auric field regularly (Reiki helps with it). Our aura's energies also represent our personality, lifestyle, thoughts, and emotions.

I've covered the various aspects of aura, including the layers, its function, aura cleansing, how to perform an aura scan, and much more ahead in the book...

Meridians

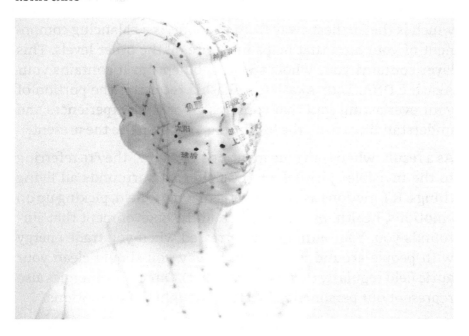

What exactly is a meridian? This is a question that every acupuncture student has when they begin their studies. A meridian is an energy highway in the human body, as per the most basic definition. They are a network of non-physical and physical channels that your life force energy (also known as Chi, Qi, or Prana) travels through. It is another energy system that connects your bodily and spiritual selves.

These meridians travel through your physical body and may get blocked, causing imbalance. Practices like Reiki and acupressure can remove these obstructions, allowing the life force energy to flow freely. Yoga and martial arts deal with this life force energy as well, helping it to flow effectively throughout the body to create balance.

Meridians occur in pairs, and each meridian has several acupuncture sites along its course. While it may be tempting to conceive about meridians in the body in the same manner that we think of the circulatory system, this is totally off base.

The meridian routes are in charge of the "distribution" of substances throughout the body, although meridians have yet to be physically defined. As a result, seeing the meridian system as an energy distribution network makes more sense.

So, how does this energy circulatory system work?

14 major meridians run throughout the body. One goes along the front center of the body, another down the spine, and the remaining 12 run from head to toe along the rest of the body. Each limb is crossed by 6 channels, 3 of which are regarded as Yin in nature and 3 of which are considered Yang in nature.

Consider various extension cables that are connected end to end and entangled. If you unraveled them, they would create a large circle. As a result, they are all linked.

The 12 Meridians are associated with various organs—the heart, lung, stomach, kidney, large intestine, small intestine, liver, bladder, gallbladder, and spleen. The other 2 meridians are the pericardium meridian, which is associated with emotional and spiritual well-being, and the triple-warmer meridian, which regulates metabolism. These are "Extraordinary" meridians that are not linked with the major organ systems. These meridians have extremely particular purposes. They serve as Qi and blood reserves. They circulate "substances" throughout the body because of their close relationship with the kidneys. They also aid in the circulation of Wei Qi, which serves as the immune system. In addition, they link the 12 regular channels.

The body stays healthy when Qi circulates freely. However, external factors like stress may cause the body's meridians to become blocked or sluggish. When there is a blockage along the meridians, the disease may set in.

Remember that these meridians link end-to-end—like extension cables—and that this is essential for the flow of your Qi. The bladder meridian, for example, travels from your eye, over your head, down your back, and all the way to your big toe, where it joins the kidney meridian. The kidney meridian then travels back up your inner legs, torso, and chest. These circuits continue to link up and down the trunk, legs, arms, and head.

The meridian system also makes use of the Yin and Yang idea to explain how Qi moves and maintains equilibrium. The Yin and Yang dualism concept can be found in everything—you can't have dark without light, or hot without cold. It's the same with your organs—you have solid "Yin" organs (heart, liver, spleen, kidney, and lungs) and hollow "Yang" organs (stomach, bladder, gallbladder, large intestine, and small intestine).

Yin and Yang are present in all living things. Yin is associated with water, darkness, and cold, while Yang is associated with fire, sunshine, and heat. The balance between Yin and Yang is required for the body to function properly.

The Yin channels are on the inner surfaces, whereas the Yang channels are on the outer surfaces. Every meridian is a Yin-Yang pair, so each Yin organ (lung, heart, kidney, liver, spleen) is linked with its equivalent Yang organ (large intestine, stomach, small intestine, bladder, gallbladder).

The meridians are also the source of energy for your muscles. Each meridian organ correlates to a muscle group—such as the kidney—which corresponds to the lower back muscles, and the small intestine, which corresponds to the quadriceps and abdominal muscles. So, if you have core weakness or difficulty ascending stairs because of leg weakness, it may be a sign that something is wrong with your small intestine and that the associated meridian is depleted of energy.

I've covered the various aspects of meridians in our body, types, how they interconnect, how they affect us, and much more later in the book...

Chakras

The energy channels in the yoga system are known as "Nadis." Think of all the Nadis or all the energy pathways in your body like the little streets, the roads, the towns that then converge into a few major cities.

Such major cities or energy hubs are called Chakras. And the Sanskrit word for chakra is called "wheel" or "disk" because these energy centers are not stagnant. They're moving. Think of each chakra as a spinning vortex of Prana (the Sanskrit word for energy) located in different sections of your spine.

The chakras begin at the base of your spine, below the pelvic region. Some claim that the 1st chakra is just partially present in the body and that it actually extends down to the ground, offering a spiritual link to the earth.

Now the chakras move up the spine from there, rising all the way up and out of the top of the head. Some say that the 7th chakra actually extends beyond the head, connecting to the sky and universal intelligence, source, energy, god, whatever you choose to call it. This is the chakra after reaching which one becomes spiritually awakened.

Chakras are the circular vortexes of energy that are placed in 7 different points on the spinal column, and all the 7 chakras are connected to the various organs and glands within the body.

These chakras are responsible for disturbing the life energy (Qi or Prana). They are virtually in the form of a fluid, and if they block and stop moving, energy cannot flow in our bodies.

It is because there is an intimate connection between the soul, mind, and the whole body. Whenever a chakra is disrupted or blocked, the life energy also gets blocked, leading to the onset of mental and health ailments.

By balancing our chakras, the water/our energies will flow more freely throughout our bodies, and thus the risk of imbalances and consequent illnesses will be reduced to a minimum.

The 7 fundamental chakras are known as Root Chakra (Muladhara), which is located at the perineum, the space between the anal outlet and the genital organ; Sacral Chakra (Svadhisthana), which is just above the genital organ; Solar Plexus (Manipuraka), which is just below the navel; Heart Chakra (Anahata), which is just beneath where the rib cage meets; Throat Chakra (Vishuddhi), which is at the pit of the throat; Third Eye (Ajna), which is between the eyebrows; and Crown Chakra (Sahasrara), also known as Brahmarandra, which is at the top of the head, where, when a child is born, there is a soft spot.

- **Root Chakra:** It is linked to survival and anchoring. It is our gateway to just about everything. Its element is the earth. It vibrates to the red color.
- **Sacral Chakra:** This chakra is linked to emotions, sexuality, and creativity. It symbolizes our one-on-one relationship with people. Water is its element. It vibrates to the orange color.
- **Solar Plexus Chakra:** This chakra is linked to individual strength, will, and self-esteem. Its element is fire. It vibrates to the yellow color.
- **Heart Chakra:** It is linked to love. Its element is air. It

vibrates to the green color.
- **Throat Chakra:** This chakra governs communication. Its element is sound. It vibrates to the blue color.
- **Third-Eye Chakra:** This chakra is linked to clairvoyance, intuition, and imagination. Its element is light. It vibrates to the indigo color.
- **Crown Chakra:** This chakra is linked with wisdom, comprehension, and awareness. Its element is thought. It resonates with the white color.

Reiki works with these three—Aura, Meridians, and Chakras—to promote physical, mental, and psychic/spiritual well-being. It helps permeate, clear, balance, and energize the whole energy body.

HOW REIKI CAN HELP WITH KUNDALINI AWAKENING?

Chakras have more than one dimension to them. One dimension is their physical existence, but they also have a spiritual dimension. Each of the 7 chakras is connected by a spiraling energy channel that climbs up the body called "Kundalini Shakti." And this entire energy system is powered by the base—the home of sexual energy. There is a tremendous amount of energy inside you that has yet to be realized. It is just waiting, since what you refer to as a human being is still in the making.

The Kundalini energy is believed to originate at the Crown Chakra and flow down to the base of the spine when we are in the womb, forming our shape and awareness. We have been trying since birth for the Kundalini to return to its natural place, transporting us back to a period when we were filled with love and amazement for everything.

Kundalini means "snake" or "serpent" energy in Sanskrit. It is the awareness' energy, a vast reservoir of creative energy believed to dwell inside the unawakened body. When it flows, it transforms your awareness.

Kundalini Awakening is described as the energy of a latent snake coiled up at the base of the spine. Consider a snake coiled eight times, ready to unleash its magnificent power at the foot of a huge mountain. She has an infinite supply of potentiating energy inside her. It is the force of creation, resting and yearning to ascend to the heights of spiritual pleasure to be in connection with awareness.

Kundalini Awakening is the process by which one transmutes his or her energy to the 7th Chakra to achieve enlightenment.

Reiki is a practice that does not require much research or the use of complicated techniques. It is a highly safe method of awakening Kundalini's energy. It is probably the only attunement technique that may open both Universal and Earth energies simultaneously, allowing the practitioner to become a highly potent conduit for healing and transformational energy.

It's not only a powerful healing technique, but it is also a personal transformation tool that may help you become conscious of the changes you want to make in your life and support you in manifesting those changes. It connects you with your Higher Self, providing you greater clarity and insights and allowing you to discover solutions inside.

The individual may promote the movement of Kundalini via a series of Reiki attunements. During the attunement, several energy centers (Chakras) and energy channels (Meridians) are opened and strengthened, allowing the individual to now channel energy via his/her own hands. Reiki restores the balance in your chakras and allows energy to flow freely throughout your body. As a result, Reiki has a cleaning and stabilizing impact, ensuring that you have more energy.

It provides us with the courage to heal, as well as insight into what we wish to create. It gives us the confidence to ask for what we desire. It also offers us the freedom to get out of our own way. Knots and blockages in the chakras are eliminated, and the body is prepared for the complete Kundalini Awakening, which occurs in line with the divine design of the soul.

Thus, when the practitioner works on himself or another person, the energy flows through at a high vibration, searching for lower energy vibrations as unresolved emotional problems, bodily obstacles and illnesses, negative thinking patterns, and outdated beliefs that no longer benefit them. This may be any kind of impediment that prevents the individual from operating effectively.

The energy channel's waking is followed by intense spiritual, mental, and bodily emotions. You feel extremely well linked to the source of life after activation.

Many individuals who practice the Reiki method have energy experiences, some of which are extremely delicate and others of which are enormously overpowering. When practitioners have an intense experience, they often inquire whether they have experienced a Kundalini experience.

Some Reiki instructors argue that this is impossible since Kundalini is not the same as Reiki. But let's take a deeper look to determine whether this is true or not.

Kundalini, according to Paramhans Swami Maheshwarananda, is "the force of the Divine Self that is concealed inside us." The term Reiki means "True Self," and the tools of the Reiki system teach us how to tap into the power of our True Self.

As a result, we may argue that it is just the language that differs, but that the substance of the two is the same; our True Self is also our Divine Self, and vice versa.

The snake and the dragon are both descended from the same source. Kundalini is often linked with a snake in Indian tradition, and a dragon in Japanese esoteric traditions. The Sanskrit term used to represent both the snake and the dragon is the same—Naga. As a result, Naga may be considered the family name of both the snake and the dragon.

Finally, we can acknowledge that the words Kundalini and Reiki both describe the same state.

THE MERIDIANS IN YOUR BODY

In the same way that Prana travels via energy channels called Nadis in the Indian Yogi tradition, Qi or Chi moves through a network of energy pathways termed 'Jing-Luo' in the Chinese tradition, which interconnects and wraps all tissues and cells. Acupuncture meridians, acupoints, and energy channels are some of the many names for them. Jing means 'to pass through,' while Luo means 'something which connects.' The term is translated as "Channels," although it is most generally known as "Meridians."

The meridians are these wonderful passageways that connect your body and all unseen parts of your life into one intercommunicating whole. Energy and blood circulate indefinitely across the meridians, while also transmitting information to and among your organs.

What sort of information is it?

They instantly send signals to increase or decrease your body temperature, indications that your body needs to release water, signals to control mood, and a plethora of other signals. Are you aware that your body is continuously talking with itself through the many signals that travel through your meridians? These vital energy channels assist organs to coordinate their activity and keep your body healthy by regulating its activities.

The meridians operate as a network, similar to a freeway system, that may be laid out throughout the body. They are analogous to the circulatory system in Western medicine, although it should be noted that meridians are not tangible.

The channel system differs from the neural system, but their flow direction is more comparable in the arms and legs than in other parts of the body. The behavior of the channels and nerve pathways is similarly comparable.

The Meridian system has a long history, dating back over 2,500 years. Traditional Chinese Medicine (TCM) is founded on the Daoist tradition, which identifies 12 major meridians and many other minor and collateral meridians.

Knowledge of the energy channels is important to both the Chinese physician and the Yogi. Most of the acupressure sites influence the main channels, and most of the Chinese medicinal herbs enter and directly affect one or more of the main channels.

While Chakras are regarded as the primary energetic centers in yoga, our internal organs are considered the main focal sites of energy storage and distribution in the Daoist paradigm.

In the human body, there are 12 main meridians. The idea of these pathways is critical to understanding the functioning and relationships of the body's organs and important chemicals. Most main meridians are named after the internal organs they affect and interact with—Qi flows via the meridian of that organ.

Understanding the effects of internal and external pathogenic elements on the body's physiological processes, as well as medical diagnosis and treatment of associated illnesses, also depends on channel knowledge.

According to the ancient Chinese classic Nei Ying Ling Shu (or "spiritual axis"), which goes back to 200-300 B.C., "it is because of the 12 main channels that people live, illness is created, people are treated, medicines function and diseases are conquered, and people die."

According to the meridians and channels hypothesis, the channels and organs are not separate entities, but rather part of a single system that works together. Both are incomprehensible as distinct entities. Organs, according to Traditional Chinese Medicine, are the gross anatomical energic functions situated at a fixed location inside the body.

Thus, the heart is regarded not just as a blood-pumping physical object situated inside the chest, but also as a component of the body-mind complex where the Shen—consciousness—is stored, generates particular emotions, such as joy, and is linked with certain sensory perception, among other things.

Channels are indeed flows of energy that goes via clearly defined routes across the body and mind, as well as inside the body. The brain is distinct from the mind. They are composed of extremely delicate materials, and their construction is quite similar to the Kundalini Yoga Nadis concept. They are less substantial and more active than organs; organs are more Yin in nature, whereas channels are more Yang.

The organs of the body may connect with the exterior environment (climate) through these meridians (channels), which assist modify the internal physiological processes in response to changes in the external climate.

Thus, meridian channels not only link the organs but also maintain them in tune with the external energies, or connect the body to the universe. For example, cold temperatures in the winter cause constriction of the arteries on the skin's surface, and the energy from the skin goes into the interiors to protect the more important organs.

Each meridian corresponds to a certain organ. The meridians go through the body along a route just under the skin, which is known as the superficial pathway.

The meridians send branches deep into the body from the surface to energize and control the activities of their respective organs. The deeper route refers to the meridian's inner portion.

Each main meridians' superficial route traverses a certain area of the body to generate its impact.

Thus, it may or may not be related to its name-bearing organ; similarly, each organ may be situated near a deep branch of a canal that does not carry the organ's name. As a result, to use acupressure methods, the meridians around the organs to be affected, even if these meridians do not directly connect to that organ, may be used.

Because of the proximity of these organs to the spleen meridian, the points on the spleen meridian may be activated to impact the liver or the intestine. Because of the interconnected structure of the meridians and their relationship to the region and organs within their vicinity, the whole body system becomes linked to each other in terms of the distribution and flow of energy, the life force.

The disease is the imbalance produced within the equilibrium of these physiological energies. Health is the creation of harmony within the energy distribution existing throughout the body.

According to TCM, your body may stay healthy as long as Qi flows freely through your meridians and your organs function in harmony. This implies that when your body's meridian system works properly, you are healthy. However, owing to a variety of factors—including excessive stress—your body's meridians may get clogged or even blocked. This impacts the operation of the associated organ and, eventually, the whole body-mind-spirit system.

Meridian-based treatments, such as Reiki, are founded on the idea that a disturbance in the flow of qi/chi energy may compromise the immune system, leaving the body vulnerable to a variety of undesirable illnesses and diseases.

Meridians Classification

The meridians are classified into two types—Jingmai and Luomai.

Jing: The Jingmai represents the majority of what is often referred to as the meridians. These travel vertically throughout the body, with the limbs going into deep tissues and bodily cavities to connect with the organs.

Luo: The Luomai are the numerous links between the Jingmai meridians. These meridians, also known as collaterals, travel horizontally and superficially throughout the body. These link the Jing meridians, as well as the connective tissues and cutaneous areas.

In the body, there are 2 centerline meridians and 12 main meridians. The meridian's name reveals which organ of the body it is closely connected to. Individual meridians have been identified and mapped throughout the body. Meridians occur bilaterally in matching pairs throughout the body. They circulate inside the body rather than on the surface. Each meridian is associated with a Yin-Yang pair (Yin being the passive female principle of the universe; Yang being the active male principle of the universe). That is, each Yin organ is coupled with its matching Yang organ, for example. The Yang Large Intestine meridian relates to the Yin Lung meridian.

The 12 meridians on each side of the body—3 Yin meridians (heart, lung, and pericardium) and 3 Yang meridians (small intestine, large intestine, and San Jiao) of the arm, 3 Yin meridians (liver, kidney, spleen), and 3 Yang meridians (urinary bladder, gallbladder, and stomach) of the leg.

Except for the one that runs down the body's median line, all the channels, both front and back, are bilateral; they are replicated on the right and left sides of the body. These meridians are classified into 6 categories based on the functions they conduct. These are the groups:

- 12 Main Channels

- 12 Transverse Luo
- 15 Longitudinal Luo
- 12 Tendino-Muscular
- 8 Extra Channels
- 12 Divergent and Extra Channels

To Visualize, picture a road map, a profusion of points woven into a web by lines of travel. Imagine this system in 3-D in your body, a huge network of invisible energy channels linking every atom, cell, tendon, bone, organ, centimeter of skin—everything in your body! They connect the top and lower portions, as well as the surface and inside so that nothing is distinct. Now, to this 3-D linked bodily "map," add additional dimensions—your mind, emotions, and spirit—everything conscious and unconscious inside you.

Unlike traditional medical systems, such as the circulatory system, conventional anatomy, and physiology have not been able to physically identify these routes. It is more helpful to think of the meridian system as an energy distribution network that is prone to energetic manifestation. Meridians are better understood as a process, as opposed to a structure.

Energy travels via meridians, allowing it to reach all areas of the body. Every organ has its own meridian, or channel, which runs through a certain region of the body. The flow of Qi in the meridians concentrates at certain locations, which are known as acupuncture points. Acupuncture sites, when needled, have been proven to affect the electrical and neurological systems of the body, influence neurotransmitters, and decrease substance P levels (which is responsible for the sensation of pain).

Apart from these vital meridians that are essential in the clinical practice of traditional Chinese medicine, there is another set of channels known as 'Tiny Channels' or 'Extraordinary Meridians' that link the tiniest and most distant regions of the body to the major channels.

The tiny channels are in charge of delivering blood, vital energy

(Chi), and other chemicals to the most inaccessible parts of the human body. As previously stated, only the 12 major meridians are important to bodily functioning and the use of treatment methods; all other meridians are subordinate to these main channels.

1. They serve as Qi and blood reservoirs for the twelve normal channels, filling and draining as needed.
2. Because they have a close link with the Kidneys, they circulate Jing or 'essence' throughout the body.
3. They aid in the circulation of defensive Wei Qi throughout the trunk of the body and therefore play a vital part in the maintenance of good health.
4. They offer additional links between the 12 regular channels.

Each unique meridian joins the other two end-to-end to create a closed circle, and all 12 major channels are linked into a circular closed circuit. As a result, these 12 major channels are always listed in the following order: -

- Lung Channel or Lu
- Colon channel, or Co., also known as the large intestine channel (L.1.)
- Stomach Channel (St.)
- Spleen Channel (Sp.)
- Heart Channel (He.)
- Small Intestine Channel (S. I.)
- Bladder Channel (Bl. or B. Or U.B.)
- Kidney Channel (Ki. or K.)
- Pericardium Channel (Pe. or P.)
- Three heater Channel (T.H.) or Triple warmer Channel (T.W.)
- Gall Bladder Channel (G.B.)
- Liver Channel (Liv.)

The names of these 12 major channels show their close connection to the function or dysfunction of the respective organs; for example, the Lung Channel is intimately related to lung functions.

The human body's meridian system is a delicate but complex network of interconnected energy channels. If a person learns this meridian system, they will grasp the mysteries of Qi energy flow in the body.

AURA CLEANSING AND REIKI

Now we know that everything in the cosmos is made of energy, which is best characterized as "information that vibrates." What's more fascinating is that everything vibrates at its own unique frequency/speed; for example, a brain cell vibrates differently than a hair cell, and similar species vibrate in similar ways but at slightly different frequencies.

Life is referred to as energy in psychology, Eastern medicine, and complementary medicine. The aura may be thought of as an energy field that surrounds the body and interacts with it on spiritual and psychological levels through chakras. In other terms, the aura is an energy field that surrounds the physical body and may be seen by individuals with psychical vision. Our aura's energies represent our personality, lifestyle, thoughts, and emotions.

You may have heard the expression "energy is contagious." All living things are sensitive entities, and it is very easy to pick up on someone's emotions and energy from casual contact with them. If someone is sending negative energy, it may adhere to you, causing intuitive blocks and emotional concerns. This is due to your aura absorbing theirs.

When we come into contact with such individuals who have a low vibration, our aura gradually weakens, and we may get fatigued or unwell. Too much negative energy will produce holes in our aura, causing energy to drain from our chakras. Aura is like a warm blanket that protects us from both physical and emotional damage. That is why they get torn and dull.

Aside from someone else's negative energy, many other factors —such as daily stress—may have an impact on your aura. You will want to guard your energy against negativity at all costs since it is critical to have cleansed channels at all times.

Aura cleansing focuses on balancing your 7 energy centers (chakras) and eliminating energy blocks that no longer serve you, allowing your energy to flow uninterrupted.

Various techniques may help cleanse your aura of negativity and previous traumas, allowing you to feel more energetic, healthy, and cheerful. Cleaning your aura of any negativity and prior traumas aids in the release of physical and emotional barriers that have been accumulated in your mind, body, and soul throughout your life, including former life traumas.

What is the Significance of the Aura?

Prana, or life force, circulates through the energy body or aura. Any disruption in this flow causes illnesses, thus keeping a healthy, clean, and vibrant aura is critical for our well-being.

If you have a problem in your physical body, it will manifest as a disruption in your energy body as well. If your liver is sluggish, this is mirrored as unclean, sticky energy in the area of your aura that corresponds to the liver.

You will have a brilliant aura if you are mentally, physically, and emotionally well, and the energy centers will be powerful and active. On the contrary, if you are lacking in any manner, your aura will be diminished, with holes and tears. You'll also be losing energy all the time, which will deplete your aura and make you worse.

Aura's Function

By filtering harmful energies, the aura shields you from the physical, emotional, and psychic energies of your surroundings (it acts as a lightning rod). The aura links you to the energy in your surroundings (it acts as an antenna or bridge). After that, the aura connects these energies to the chakras and other energy pathways like meridians (which further process them, often resulting in nerve, hormonal, vascular, and other activity in the physical body).

The aura emits signals into your surroundings that convey information about you and attract particular forms of energy to you. It contains a network of interconnected fields that serve as blueprints for your physical body, emotions, awareness, relationships, and growth. The 7 main chakras have their origins in the physical body, but they may also be found at all levels of the aura. With each level, the energy's pace and vibration level increase. Each layer corresponds to the chakra with the same number.

Layers of Aura

The human aura is a multi-layered energy field. It is made up of 7 auric layers (also known as bodies or planes), each of which reflects a distinct aspect of the universe. Consider them to be the layers of an onion, with the center representing your physical body.

Auras may stretch up to 4 feet out from the body. Each auric layer corresponds to one of the 7 chakras.

The 7 layers are:

1. Etheric Aura
2. Emotional Aura
3. Mental Aura
4. Astral Aura
5. Etheric Template Aura

6. Celestial Aura
7. Ketheric Aura

1. The Etheric Aura

It is the layer that is nearest to your skin. This normally extends approximately 2 inches beyond the actual body and is blue in color. This aura is linked to the body's health and physical state.

2. Emotional Aura

It is related to emotion. If you're caught up in your emotions, this plane will reveal it. It changes hue based on your mood and will seem dull or smear if you're going through a rough patch emotionally. Positive emotions emit brilliant colors, whilst negative emotions emit dark colors.

This is around 2-4 inches away from the physical body. This aura manifests itself as rainbow-colored clouds.

3. Mental Aura

It is the 3rd layer that protrudes from your body. This is around 4-8 inches away from the physical body. It has a yellow color. It is linked to our reasoning, logic, thoughts, and mental processes. When we are thinking, our Mental Aura seems bright.

4. Astral Aura

This plane is concerned with your spiritual well-being. It's also where you keep your love capacity. This is around 8-12 inches away from the physical body. This may also be seen as rainbow-colored clouds. It serves as a link between the physical and spiritual domains.

5. Etheric Template Aura

It stabilizes the Etheric Aura. This is where your psychic skills are revealed. A clean etheric plane allows you to tap into other people's energy and connect with individuals who are on the same wavelength as you.

This is in blue color that stretches 12-24 inches from the actual body.

6. Celestial Aura

This is the plane where you hold your dreams and instincts. It's also the plane of enlightenment; people with a strong Celestial Aura plane are usually very creative.

It extends to about 24 inches from the physical body and looks like a shimmering light of bright colors.

7. Ketheric Template Aura

This is the last plane of the aura. It balances out all the other planes and ultimately helps lead you on your life's journey. It safeguards everything inside its boundaries.

It stretches 36-48 inches from the physical body and looks like a dazzling golden light. Beyond this level is the cosmic plane.

What Do Their Different Hues Mean?

Your aura's hues correlate to one of the 7 major chakras—Root, Sacral, Solar Plexus, Heart, Throat, Third Eye, and Crown. Knowing which colors belong to particular chakras might assist you in interpreting what your aura is saying to you.

Red

The color red resonates in your Root Chakra. It is located at the base of your spinal column and houses your fundamental concerns—such as who you are, your home, your profession, your manifesting abilities, sexual energy, and your values.

If your aura comprises red, it signifies you're operating from a stable foundation.

Orange

Orange represents your Sacral Chakra, which is situated in your lower belly. It includes the emotional body's initial vitality, creativity, the capacity to reach out to others in relationships, and sexual energy.

If you have an orange aura, it means you're feeling the emotional equivalent of curling up beneath a weighted blanket. You're also self-sufficient and realistic.

Yellow

Yellow is associated with your Solar Plexus Chakra. This chakra is located a few inches above the belly button. It is the home of your individuality, personal strength, identity, and emotions. It defines who you are to yourself and the rest of the world. Yellow auras indicate you are creative, inquisitive, and cheerful.

Pink and Green

These colors are associated with your Heart Chakra. It should come as no surprise that your Heart Chakra is all about love—both for others and for yourself. It is the home of compassion and the power of forgiveness. It also grants access to the divine mind and intuition. These pink or green aura hues are associated with compassion, kindness, and love.

Blue

The color blue represents your Throat Chakra. It's your way of being yourself, expressing what you need to say, and interacting with yourself and others. Blue auras indicate you are perceptive and sympathetic.

Violet and Purple

Purple is associated with your Third Eye Chakra, which you're certainly acquainted with if you've done yoga. It's in the middle of your forehead, above your physical eyes. It is your vision of everything you want to accomplish, as well as the source of your intuition. You may discover that you have psychic abilities and are very perceptive.

White

White auras are quite uncommon. This hue resonates in your Crown Chakra, which is positioned above your head. It binds you to All That Is, Oneness, and the realization that we are all interconnected.

Black

If your aura seems black, it indicates that you are hanging on to certain bad thoughts and emotions that are obstructing the passage of energy through your chakras.

How to Determine Your Aura State?

Aura scanning can be majorly beneficial when trying to figure out the state of your aura. A scan might assist in revealing the various colors of your existing aura and pinpoint any issues. It may reveal your energy levels, any harm to your energy flow, and any chakra imbalances. Aura scans may be conducted in person or remotely.

The scan is carried out by a Reiki practitioner who can detect auras either visually or by a kinaesthetic technique in which the individual may detect auras. New technology also allows for aura scanning cameras. These cameras can display your aura in color and assist you in visualizing your energy.

If you want to perform it yourself, simply close your eyes and focus your attention on your feet. Slowly, move upward till head and try to notice any blockage or discomfort in any area. The other way is to focus on any symptoms that relate to the unbalanced chakra. Once figured out, choose the appropriate crystal and proceed with the practice.

You can master the art of recognizing auras and comprehending various colors and energies by practicing Reiki daily.

Signs that You Need to Cleanse Your Aura

Though you should always be aware when you are stuck in a negative cycle, in case you have missed the warning signals, here is some assistance. Maybe you don't believe in bad vibes at all, but if you encounter any of these indicators, there's a good probability you're trapped in one and need to be cleansed.

- If you're having a horrible day or are in a state of despair.
- If you're depressed for no apparent cause.
- If you are ill or under stress.
- If you have constant fights with family/loved ones.
- If you feel stuck in your life.

The Benefits of Aura Cleansing

Maintaining a clean and flowing aura may be helpful on many levels. You may live a more balanced life if you have a positive aura. Here are some advantages of aura cleansing:

- It improves your energy by reducing lethargy and improving creativity.
- Improved creativity eases boredom and a sense of being lost.
- Enhances motivation.
- Release body aches and pains.
- You feel more connected in everything you do.
- You find safety and comfort in your own skin.
- Releases energy blockages caused by trauma in both the current and previous lives.

- Balances your energy centers (chakras) and dispel bad energy.

How Reiki Affects the Aura?

We are all interconnected in this universe, and our auras, are continually interacting with the energy fields of other creatures and the environment. Aura cleansing can rapidly and effectively remove energetic obstructions from all levels of the energy field. These obstructed patterns might be current, from childhood, or a previous life.

For example, if you feel exhausted or overwhelmed at huge gatherings or with specific individuals, you have felt this connection. Your aura, or energy field, picks up on other people's energy.

Interactions with other beings, as well as our physical surroundings—electromagnetic pollution, air quality, water quality, the food we consume, and our own emotional state—all impact our energy field.

We take care of our physical bodies most of the time by exercising, drinking lots of clean water, and eating good foods; but we also need to take care of our energy bodies regularly. Aura cleansings aid in the purification of our energies and resolving concerns that we carry from life to life.

Reiki influences the aura bodies. Aura cleansing via Reiki is a powerful technique that may interrupt the pattern of repetitive thoughts, actions, and negativity that we humans believe we must carry with us every day. There are various Reiki techniques that may help align your aura and ensure a healthy flow of energy to and from your aura. It helps to boost the practitioner's aura and gives him control over his life.

Reiki will work on the outer aura and relieve blockages and cleanse the chakras, allowing the body, mind, and soul link to be unified as it should be. You get the confidence to take control of your life and growth via Reiki attunements and aura strengthening.

During the session, we identify and extract the root cause of any problem—such as unworthiness, wrath, fear, uncertainty, helplessness, and others. After you have extracted the underlying cause(s) from your energy body, you may simply create new patterns in dealing with residual emotions as they arise. A 30-minute session leaves you feeling balanced, rejuvenated, and replenished.

Before a Reiki attunement, a person's aura may only extend a few centimeters beyond the person's body. The attunement increases the aura's intensity and gives it a radius of around 2-5 meters. Simultaneously, mindfulness, inner vitality, and the ability to instinctively perceive what has to be altered to reach optimal health are enhanced.

Other Ways to Purify Your Aura

1. Imagine Divine white light engulfing your whole body and traveling through all of your chakras, from the Crown to the Root, eradicating any bad energy from your aura and chakras.

2. Draw all the attuned symbols on your hands, then comb your fingers from head to toe to eliminate any negativity from aura and throw them into a violet flame. This process should be repeated 5 times.

3. After combing, envision a white light as a ball in your palms and move from head to toe saying "Reiki I am pasting the auras of... (myself or your knowable's name)." All the gaps in the aura will be filled with this practice.

4. Soak the negative energy removal crystals in water overnight, then remove them and charge the water with Reiki to clear any bad energy. When you return home from the outdoors, shower

with this water from head to toe. You will get a sense of serenity and relaxation.

5. Shielding is another easy and efficient approach for protecting oneself from energy drain.

6. One more way is to use an amulet with the Reiki intention slip to protect yourself from bad energies.

TREATING ENERGY BLOCKS IN YOUR MIND AND BODY

Energy is a tangible, animating life force that we can all comprehend in terms of how we feel daily (sluggish, over-tired, or on the flip side, invincible). We usually blame low energy levels on a lack of sleep or poor nutrition. But it's a lot more complex than that.

Molecules make up everything. Even something as substantial as a table is always vibrating, and we, as humans, are also vibrating.

When we say something has positive vibes, we are referring to the vibrating energy of the individual. People that are happy vibrate at a higher frequency.

Even locations have their own feel. When you enter a room where a violent fight has occurred, you may sense the thick energy and may want to leave immediately. Because of the salt and flowing air, beaches have a light vibe. The air near the beach vibrates at a higher frequency as well.

Tell me, do even the littlest comments irritate you? Have you been too fatigued recently? Do you find yourself uninterested in your relationships? Because your aura and chakras or energy centers are blocked, you may suffer all these symptoms.

When the energy circuit that runs through our system becomes stuck, our energy levels drop, we feel achiness or stiffness, and our attention is hampered.

The human body requires energy to maintain its different functions and to assist the person in carrying out his or her chosen activities. This energy is derived from the food we eat. When we eat, we are absorbing energy or assimilating energy, or 'energy in,' and when we work, exercise, or engage in any physical activity, we are dissipating energy or sending out energy, or 'energy out.'

Because the rates at which our body dissipates and absorbs energy are not always the same, the body can store energy for future use. The stored energy is usually in the form of fat or white adipose tissue. When the rates of energy intake and expenditure are fairly healthy, there is less energy stored, resulting in a healthy energy balance. When these rates are significantly divergent, the body is considered to be in an energy imbalance.

Blocked Energy

When our energy is balanced, our minds are open and flexible, our breath is deep and rhythmic and we have a sense of spaciousness in our bodies. We keep a healthy balance of expansion and contraction, as well as activation (doing) and receptivity (being/allowing) while we are in the flow. We let our reason (thinking), emotion (feeling), and will (doing) to collaborate. Plus, we believe in ourselves and the process, and we are properly undefended. This is referred to as being in energy integrity.

Most individuals I know, including myself, find these bursts of energy to be fleeting. Many people's energy is frequently described as being obstructed, sluggish, or trapped. Their thinking is rigid and limited. Their breathing is shallow, paused, or irregular, and specific muscles are stiff or weak. They feel ungrounded, over-bound (separate), under-bound (enmeshed), or fractured energetically.

They struggle to strike a good balance between doing and

being, giving and receiving. They may be either aggressive or submissive. They are either excessively rational, overly passionate, or too determined. They battle obstinacy, procrastination, perfectionism, compulsive thinking, excessive individuality, or conformity.

Examples of energetic blocks include:

Cognitive Blocks

A closed mind is an energy hindrance. We are stuck when our belief system is fixed. "This is simply how it is," or "I'm just not that type of person," or "God doesn't want me to have that," I often hear. These are cognitive blocks.

Forcing Currents

Our energy is hindered when we lack confidence in the process or in ourselves. We are unable to turn our will over in this situation. There is no surrender in this situation. Instead, we focus our attention on circumstances or people because we don't trust that we'll receive what we need—we think that the only way in is to push our way in. Our energy grasp is strong and dominating, creating demands like "give it to me" or "I will make you adore me." This is referred to as a forcing current of energy.

Signs Your Chakras/Energy Centers are Blocked:

- Digestion concerns
- Toxins
- Shocks—whether emotional, physical, or mental
- Other invasive treatments, such as surgery
- Environmental pollutants—including mobile phones, computers, radiation, microwaves, and so on
- Physical injury
- Nutritional deficiencies
- Poor standard of living and a lack of support
- Long-term usage of pharmaceuticals

- Abuse of drugs and alcohol
- Childbirth difficulty
- Situations that cause vulnerability, anxiety, loss, and sorrow
- Feeling easily overburdened
- Difficulty making minor choices
- Relationship issues
- Tiredness
- A lack of self-esteem
- Difficulties receiving or expressing love/affection to others
- Interdependence
- Shyness and passivity
- Feelings of anxiety, worry, or depression
- A lack of life direction
- A sense of lack of control over your life
- Difficulty advocating for oneself
- Brain Fog
- Poor problem-solving ability

What Causes Energy Blocks?

Chakras constantly filter energy into and out of the body. Worry and stress in our everyday lives affect our Chakras, causing them to get blocked, preventing energy from flowing freely through our bodies.

If any of the chakras become clogged or totally blocked, the fresh, positive, balanced energy required by the mind, body, and soul to operate correctly cannot circulate efficiently throughout our bodies. Chakra and energy flow blockages may result in a range of emotional, behavioral, and physical problems. Energy healing aims to clear up any congestion or blockages in the chakras, bringing the mind, body, soul, earth, health, universality, and grounding into a healthy state of balance.

Blockages or negative energy may occur as a result of traumatic life events, stress, disease, emotional difficulties, or environmental causes. This may result in tiredness, cognitive fog, sickness, or simply a general sense of being off balance. The negative aura that cannot leave the body also clogs the chakras. The chakras get cleaned, aligned, and balanced by Reiki and promote better health.

The following are some of the potential causes of your energy blockage:

You May Be Trying to Dodge Something

It's likely you've been avoiding it because you're going through a tough period emotionally, professionally, financially, or in some other manner. Facing difficult circumstances straight on is never fun, but postponing your reaction to whatever it is may prolong—or worsen—the problem.

For example, if you're scared to confront someone who has harmed you, energy blockages may form and create a variety of additional issues—such as sleeplessness, headaches or migraines, chest discomfort, or bodily tension. You're also unlikely to get relief if you attempt to mask the symptoms with medicines without treating the underlying cause.

Emotions and Trauma Suppression

It is critical that we identify, express, and let go of our unpleasant feelings. It is difficult to confront unpleasant feelings straight on. Most of us do our best to avoid them. This is why the most frequent energy block is repressing emotions and trauma. However, it is critical to your health and well-being on all levels—physically, mentally, and spiritually. If you don't process your pain, it will return or you will turn it inside against yourself. This wrath, fear, guilt, or worry will alter Ki, resulting in bodily symptoms like digestion problems, sleeplessness, and tiredness.

You're Under Stress or Overworked

As much as most of us would want to believe that we can accomplish anything and everything at peak performance all the time, it is just not feasible, or healthy. Overworking and/or being in a high-stress state 24 hours a day is a quick and definite way to create energy blockages, leaving us tired, uninspired, and irritated.

Permitting Other People Energies to Overpower Yours

You've probably encountered bad energy from other people's aura if you've ever gone into a room and sensed the tension in the air. When you don't know how to shield yourself from other people's energy, you absorb it as if it were your own. And you start to feel like the bad energy you've absorbed. Most of us aren't even aware that this is occurring. Boundaries are required to prevent the energy of others from mixing with your own. When your boundaries are weak, unprotected, or unclear, you let all kinds of energy and emotions to enter that isn't yours. Furthermore, you unintentionally give up your own energy to others, leaving you exhausted or stressed.

Not Taking Care of Yourself

Even if you have a lot on your plate, practicing self-care is one way to keep possible energy blockages at bay.

If you've stopped eating healthily, skipped the gym or other kinds of exercise, or remained up late working on assignments several nights in a row, you're probably not allowing enough time to concentrate on yourself. Self-care may look different for you than it does for someone else, but the key is to discover what works for you (meal planning, yoga, meditation, journaling, sleeping in, etc.) and include it in your weekly, if not daily, routine.

You Become Your Suffering

You are not your sickness or suffering. Doctors and experts may name your suffering, but this does not define who you are. It may raise questions about what you can accomplish and how you can do it, but that's all. You can remove the label and restore your True Self.

Question Yourself! Ask whether you are the sensation or you are having the sensation (you're not the sensation, you are the one experiencing it, you're the experiencer!). Determine what is true for you and take action. It's never pleasant to be in pain or struggle. However, it is a chance to address the underlying source of your symptoms and feel better.

You are Harbouring Bad Energy

Anger, heartbreak, worry, dread, and regret. Negative energy has hundreds of different faces, and it is a major source of energy blockages.

This goes beyond just avoiding what we mentioned before. Even after a scenario has played out fully, we may unconsciously hang on to unpleasant thoughts or sentiments. This may happen because we've become used to it as a terrible habit, or because we're unsure how to let it go. However, if it persists for too long, your aura may get affected, preventing good energy from flowing and negatively affecting our general well-being.

Prioritizing Your Needs Lastly

The house has to be cleaned, the meeting needs to be planned, the kids need assistance with their schoolwork, and the dog needs to be groomed. It seems like we are all moving at a breakneck pace. But where do your requirements fit in? We often use more energy than we get. You may do this because you believe that attending to your own needs is selfish and that your needs are somehow less essential. This is entirely false!

If you neglect yourself for a long enough period of time, blockages in your energy pathways will form, and your body will alert you that you need to slow down and pay attention.

I've found that the secret to self-care is first identifying what makes you happy and then doing more of it. Get used to expressing "I need..." and speak freely about what matters to you and what hurts your emotions when you are ignored or disrespected. This does not imply that you are unconcerned about others. Quite the contrary. You're taking care of yourself so that you can be your best for everyone else.

Denial of Your Ture Self

Life may get away from us at times. You go to college, choose a degree that will give a steady salary, marry, have children, and BOOM! You glide through life's milestones feeling nothing. And you wonder, "Why am I unhappy?" or "How did I end myself here?" These thoughts are easily dismissed since there is always someone or something else that requires your attention.

When you disregard yourself and your real goals, you give up on what is most important to you. You must first listen to that voice in your mind if you want to know who you really are at your heart. That voice is your intuition, or "gut feeling," and it serves as your guide. When your energy is trapped in avoidance or fear, you become detached from your innermost aspirations, and your inner voice becomes muffled and difficult to hear.

Accept and connect with what you're feeling. You have the right to live your life as you see fit. The first step in removing this energy barrier is to spend time getting to know yourself, your values, and your aspirations. Recognize and nourish your True Self.

Ask yourself the following probing questions, then write down your heartfelt responses. Write the answers that are required of you beforehand if it helps. Then go through the questions again. Once you've found genuine answers to these questions, decide on one modest action you can do today to align yourself with your unique life mission.

1. Who are you really and what's your purpose here?

2. What is that you love doing?
3. What do you want to leave behind before you die?

Restoring Energetic Integrity

It is clear from the above that energy blockages are harmful to one's health. Depending on your priorities at the moment, it's a good idea to get started on energy healing.

The restoration of energy integrity requires some self-exploration, as well as the willingness to invest time and risk. The task at hand requires us to perform the effort to become more aware. It requires us to accept responsibility for how we spend our energy to protect and keep ourselves apart. It invites us to get acquainted with our belief systems and the pictures we regard as absolutes. And it invites us to feel into our bodies and energies, seeing where we distort and where we fail to bring life to.

Pieces of the jigsaw will start to fall into place as you become more aware of your energy. You may begin to see how you utilize your energy to protect yourself from particular events and feelings. You may see how your energy has been used as a part of an adaptive strategy, how it has benefited you, and how it no longer serves you. You will hopefully begin to see how using your energy in this manner prevents you from realizing the full potential of your life force.

This process isn't only for our own personal development. If we can comprehend the connection between our own energy and awareness, we may grasp the relationship between energy and consciousness in the systems in which we live—such as our families, our political system, money, war, and how we treat our planet. What if we regarded war, for example, as an energy distortion of power and creativity? What if we saw the obsessive pursuit of economic riches as a cognitive distortion of safety and scarcity/abundance?

Energetic distortions may be found nearly everywhere in our

society and ourselves, and they are sustained by our lack of awareness. We have a fair chance of changing ourselves and the society we live in if we can comprehend the distortion of energy and undertake the hard work to convert it back to its natural flow.

Helpful Hints for Understanding Your Energy System:

Please keep in mind that this is a process of becoming conscious. You can't accomplish everything all at once, so have an open mind and be ready to take things slowly.

- **Recognize Your Thoughts:** Begin with your first thought of the day and work your way up. Make a list of everything. Take note of your wording and if your thinking is definite (this is how it is) or flexible (this is how it could be).
- **Simply Come to a Halt Over the Course of Your Day:** Shut your eyes. Go inside and get a sense of where you are. Do you feel in the moment? What is the composition of your breath? Are you still holding it? How do you feel in your own skin? Restricted? Relaxed? Are you exhausted and collapsing? Are you awake and alert?
- **Move:** Get your body moving. At the same time, different parts. What happens when you change your position? Take note of any thoughts or emotions that arise. Is there any area of your body that, when stimulated by movement, makes you feel something? Do you feel the urge to contain your energy or do you let it flow?
- **Make a Noise:** Allow your voice to be heard, whether alone or with others. Boost the power of your "Yes" and "No." Check to see whether one is easier than the other. Are you even willing to create a noise? Simply observe without passing judgment.
- **Introspect:** Where in your life are there strong currents? Where do you sense constant pressure on your-

self or others? Where do you impose your will on people or situations? What happens to your energy when you're in the company of others? Take careful notice of your breathing and your body. Do you like to grow or contract?

- **Experiment with Limits:** Find a buddy that is ready to push their energy limits. Keep a certain space between you. As one of you approaches the other, pay attention to when you sense their energy. Examine what occurs to you when someone else's energy enters your own energy field. Do you ever lose yourself? Do you have a sense of being unmoored? Do you believe you have the authority to raise your voice and urge her or him to move closer or farther away?
- **Make a List of Your Emotions:** Associate with each emotion. What is your connection with that feeling? What are your thoughts or pictures regarding such emotions? Where, if anywhere, do you experience those emotions in your body? Where do you feel most at ease meeting the rest of the world?
- **Figure Your Nature:** Do you lead with logic (thinker), emotion (feeler), or willpower (doer)? How do you feel about the others if you lead with one? What portions of your body do you use to interact with the outside world? Your mind, heart, and hands?
- **Experiment:** Seek other people's experiences with your energy and pay attention to the energy of others. How do you feel in their company? Are you welcomed or held at bay? Do you get the impression that they hold back, hold in, hold up, collapse, or disperse their energy? Tune in and immerse yourself in it. Feel things out rather than trying to figure it out.

How Does Reiki Help with It?

People may benefit from energy healing to relax and enhance their quality of life. Energy healing is a holistic technique that aids in the activation of the body's subtle energy systems to eliminate blockages. By breaking down these energy barriers, the body's natural capacity to repair itself is activated.

The human body is a full energy system that is in sync with the rest of the Universe. Any imbalance in the body causes a blockage in the flow of energy, resulting in disease. Energy healing ensures that the energy exchange inside the body is unimpeded. Music therapy, Reiki, and therapeutic touch are the most common forms of energy treatment.

Regular Reiki treatment creates a constant and unlocked flow of energy throughout the body. This reduces stress, improves learning and memory, increases mental clarity, and promotes physical healing/less physical discomfort. When energy pathways are obstructed, good energy cannot reach certain areas of the body, resulting in mood swings, anxiety, rage, pain, and other symptoms. Reiki may help keep these passageways clean.

When energies flow freely, your body can establish internal equilibrium and remove imbalances caused by unwanted influences. No chakra functions effectively in isolation from the others; they are all interconnected. Only until all the chakras are completely aligned and engaged with the energy system can each chakra function effectively.

When the mind, body, and soul are in sync, the biological intelligence that controls the body's resources and enables it to recover and operate properly is amplified. As a result, Reiki is the key that unlocks the body's full potential.

Also, you do not need to be spiritual to benefit from energy healing/Reiki. It's best to walk in with an open mind for the best results, and you may see an energy healer at any time.

An energy healing session may help you relax and feel more balanced, whether you are worried, agitated, or physically exhausted. And even if you're already feeling well, there's always the possibility of feeling even better.

STEP-BY-STEP REIKI HEALING

It's tempting to dwell on big decisions and how they changed your life, yet the significant decisions we make in life are decided by our daily choices, such as the decision to practice Reiki self-healing.

The simplicity of Reiki practice is one of its distinguishing features. It is simple to learn and practice self-care by anybody interested, regardless of age or health. Children, as well as the elderly and infirm, may learn to practice. To gain insight, no prior background or certificates are required.

Everyone can assess Reiki's energy. As an example, simply rub your hands together rapidly for a few seconds, then keep them firm an inch or two apart. Feel the sensation of buzzing in your hands. Put your hands over your eyes and feel how warm they are. This delicate energy is your life force—your true human superpower. Reiki practice (or sending Reiki out of your hands and into your body's chakras) may help you truly come to know/make a link with your power.

Of course, it's subtle. Much more subtle than a coffee rush or a gust of chilly wind. But, in my experience, connecting with that super-subtle energy is often the medication we need when we're feeling very depleted.

Note: Self-healing with Reiki is similar to meditation, you may modify your approaches to what works best for you. It is ultimately up to us, like with any type of healing, to do the work. We must assist ourselves in healing and allow it to occur. Remember, there are as many approaches to do it as there are Reiki practitioners. The ideal approach to practice is obviously the way you will practice. Reiki practice isn't theoretical; it's practical.

Some Suggestions to Help You Prepare for Your Reiki Practice

1. Remind yourself, before you begin, that Reiki is the universal life force energy that already exists inside everyone. Reiki energy boosts the body's inherent healing capabilities.

2. Practitioners are advised to practice their Reiki self-treatment whether or not they are feeling good. Consider your Reiki self-treatments to be unique moments throughout the day when you may be tranquil and calm.

3. Make it a habit to practice your Reiki self-treatments at the same time every day. It is recommended that you begin your day with a 20-minute self-treatment and then follow up with another 20-minute self-treatment at the end of the day. These treatments may be done for extended periods if desired (30-60 minutes). The time of day may also be changed to suit your needs.

4. Create a secure and comfortable environment in your house for self-care. Attempt to return to this location regularly. These self-treatments may be done while sitting in a chair or while laying on your back on a couch, bed, or the floor.

5. Unless you need the presence of another person in the room for your care and safety, try practicing self-healing alone in the room.

6. Establish a calm atmosphere free of distracting sounds. Many people find it helpful to listen to calming instrumental music while self-treating (I don't recommend it).

7. When you're ready to begin your Reiki session, head to your designated space, put on some calming background music (optional), and take off your shoes. Place a pillow under your head and a rolled-up second cushion under your legs if you are reclining. To keep warm, wrap a blanket over your body. Shut your eyes. Relax your whole body and mind. Make a mental note of any specific areas of your body or mind that need extra attention throughout your session. Remind yourself that your Reiki self-treatment is for your highest and best benefit. Awake your energy via Reiki meditation and proceed with the session. During your session, take slow, soothing breaths. It might be beneficial to concentrate on your breath and body as you go through the different hand positions.

Some Practices to Cultivate Serene and Peaceful Aura in the Environment

Aromatherapy

Aromatherapy may be used to enhance Reiki sessions. Reiki with essential oils may be quite calming. Many individuals get so calm that they go into a near-sleep state and must be gently roused up when the session is over.

Reiki will always work for the greatest good, thus when combined with the energy found in essential oils, it will direct the energy to where it is most needed and will do the most benefit. Essential oils have powerful fragrances that may transport us from the present to the past, sparking our basic instincts and transporting us back to crucial times in our life.

Furthermore, Reiki healing and essential oils are an effective combo for unblocking energy pathways that run between your chakras.

Create an aromatherapy mix to spray around the room while the Reiki treatment is being done by using essential oils in a diffuser in the area where the Reiki treatment will be administered.

Before you begin Reiki, sample a variety of oils and pick one that appeals to you because it reminds you of a previous happy event or a childhood memory, to add even more joy and relaxation to your Reiki treatment experience.

There are several oils that may be used in Reiki treatments for various purposes; however, here are a few of the most common and efficient essential oils used in Reiki sessions.

1. Patchouli

The color red represents the 1st chakra (Root Chakra). A balanced Root Chakra will allow you to remain grounded, providing you with stability, stillness, prosperity, physical health, a feeling of safety and personal security, a sense of belonging, and the capacity to live in the moment (mindfulness).

If the Root Chakra is out of balance or blocked, your physical body becomes stuck in the moment rather than being in the moment on a continuous journey, resulting in fear and self-loathing as well as hatred and anger towards your own body. Other issues can include a poor relationship with money and reliance on outside influences rather than becoming self-sovereign. The Root Chakra may be brought back into balance by combining Reiki with Patchouli, giving you a feeling of personal sovereignty and a grounded attitude to life and the people around you.

2. Neroli

The orange color represents the 2nd chakra (sacral). It denotes energy, self-fulfillment, and sexual desire, and it is associated with the sacral vertebra and reproductive organs, affecting circulation, urine function, and reproduction.

Neroli is beneficial in removing any energy blocks from Sacral Chakra. A balanced Sacral Chakra allows you to appreciate life and accept pleasure and happiness. It also improves emotional intelligence, sexual fulfillment, desire, and the capacity to accept our ever-changing reality.

Sexual dissatisfaction, difficulty in creating meaningful connections, lack of interest in sexual experiences, toxic relationships, and a negative self-image may all come from a blocked or imbalanced Sacral Chakra.

3. Pine

The color yellow stimulates the 3rd chakra (Solar Plexus), which influences your connection with yourself. A properly balanced Solar Plexus Chakra gives you a feeling of your own strength and ability, which you may use for good. It also allows you to be inspired by others, recognize them, and follow in their footsteps without feeling envious.

A blocked or imbalanced Solar Plexus Chakra might result in you giving up your talents and abilities to others because you believe it is the only way to be loved, as well as anxiety and stomach issues and putting your aspirations on wait owing to poor self-esteem. Balance may be regained by combining Pine with Reiki.

4. Rosewood

The 4th chakra (Heart Chakra) represents spirituality, compassion, emotion, love, and forgiveness and is symbolized by the color green. A healthy Heart Chakra provides emotional stability as well as the capacity to love both others and oneself. It also offers you the capacity to lessen the sorrow of others by being a good listener and showing and acting compassionately.

Difficulties with giving or receiving love, hanging on to previous unpleasant experiences, carrying grudges, heart problems, and fear of commitment to others are all signs of a blocked or imbalanced Heart Chakra.

5. Lavender

This fragrance oil is incredibly beneficial for the 5th chakra (Throat Chakra), which is symbolized by the colors blue or turquoise and, when blocked, may create difficulties with communication and expressing oneself. It is associated with the throat, esophagus, and shoulders, arms, and neck.

An unobstructed and balanced Throat Chakra allows you to express yourself and interact with others freely, while a blocked fifth chakra causes you to fear the world and leads you to withdraw from society and others.

6. Sandalwood

The Third Eye is the 6th chakra. When the Third Eye gets blocked or imbalanced, it might impair your ability to read others accurately. It allows you to glimpse what is possible. It opens your mind to the possibility of having aspirations that might lead to personal achievement. It also provides you the capacity to see through dishonest and deceptive individuals who might do you damage; the Third Eye is your intuition, and it is crucial in keeping you safe.

This oil promotes self-awareness and the capacity to tune in to your surroundings. Inability to focus, difficulties visualizing a hopeful future, and narrow-mindedness are all signs that your third eye is obstructed or imbalanced.

7. Lime

This oil is beneficial to the 7th chakra (Crown Chakra), which is symbolized by the color violet. It denotes self-awareness, willpower, and heavenly connection. It has links to the pineal gland, pituitary gland, cerebral cortex, and cerebrum. The Crown Chakra links you to the outside world, assisting you in gathering new information and keeping your mind open to the possibilities of the cosmos and the world around you.

It also allows you to open up and let the divine spirit lead you to contentment and ultimate self-knowledge. Aligning yourself with the material world rather than the spiritual world, loneliness, anger, and the sensation of being alienated from the world around you are all symptoms of a blocked or imbalanced Crown Chakra.

Candles

A candle is one of the most beautiful and soothing things a Reiki practitioner can use. The flame of a candle soothes our soul, lowering tension and promoting self-awareness. The soothing illumination allows us to relax and perhaps enter a meditative state.

Candle healing sends forth incredibly pure, delicate, and loving energies. Of course, a beeswax candle is preferable to a paraffin candle, but both are equally effective.

Also, when we wish to transmit continual healing, candle healing is the best option. When a person is very sick, candles may guarantee Reiki is transmitted throughout the night and, if necessary, throughout the day.

Simply pick some candles and light them before beginning your healing to witness the magic for yourself.

Reiki Healing Steps

Step 1: Embracing the Principles

A Reiki healing session can't proceed without embracing the 5 principles. These principles assist you in letting go and receiving whatever energy you need right now for your best welfare; the principles assist you in returning home, back to your spiritual home, and back into balance. And they may be used for more than just Reiki sessions; they can also be utilized as a morning intention or anytime you need them.

In prayer pose, repeat these principles. You may either say them out or repeat them in your head. Feel these principles while you're speaking.

1. Just for Today, I Release Angry Thoughts
2. Just for Today, I Release Thoughts of Worry
3. Just for Today, I'm Grateful
4. Just for Today, I Expand My Consciousness
5. Just for Today, I'm Gentle with All Beings
6. Conclude the principles with some prayers. You can say something like, "Oh Lord Buddha, Oh Reiki Energy, Oh The Supreme Powers, Bless Us, Bless Us, Bless Us…"

If you like, you may even create your own set of principles.

Step 2: Awakening the Energy via Reiki Meditation (Gassho)

Obviously, energy is required for energy healing. The resource is inside you; all you need is a spark to ignite your energy and allow the cosmos to do its work. Reiki meditation will help you with this.

Connecting to our energy source is a vital element of taking care of our bodies and minds. Allowing time to activate our energy centers consciously provides us with an exceptional opportunity to call abundance into our lives. It may help you sense and activate the universal energy in your body, which can provide you with a lot of healing.

Plato (Athenian philosopher, 428-347 B.C.) believed that the whole healing process must include a "soul" component and that our body, mind, and spirit must be treated and cured holistically. Reiki works in the same way!

Reiki Meditation is further divided into 4 steps:

1. Prepare

Sit back in a straight-backed chair or cross-legged, whatever is most comfortable for you. Set an intention for your Reiki practice by bringing your hands to your heart. Something like, "I'd want to feel anchored in my body."

Shut your eyes and take a few deep breaths. Then, repeat the word 'OM' 3 times.

2. Relax

Take a long, deep breath. Close your eyes and witness the sounds. Do not try to identify them. Tell yourself that your senses are relaxing.

It's time to unwind your mind. Inhale deeply through your nose and exhale through your mouth. Continue to breathe deeper and deeper like this 3 times. Slowly count down from 10 to 1 to enter a deeper state of relaxation.

Now perform a body scan. Relax your body's organs one by one. While relaxing, thank them for their help and ask them to continue to help you healthily for the rest of your life.

Relax the right toes, right foot, right ankle, right leg, right knee, right thigh, and right hip.

Relax the left foot, left ankle, left leg, left knee, left thigh, and left hip.

Relax your pelvic area and the organs inside it. Relax the back muscles, the abdomen, the stomach, the liver on the right side, and the spleen on the left, then the gallbladder, pancreatic bowels, and kidneys in the back.

Relax your chest, heart, and lungs. Feel how serene they are. Relax the whole rib cage as well as the shoulder blades. Feel them fully relax.

Relax the right shoulder, upper arm, right elbow, forearm, right hand, and fingers.

Now relax the left shoulder, upper arm, elbow, forearm, hand, and fingers. Your left upper limb, from the shoulder to the fingers, is now completely relaxed.

Relax the front and rear neck muscles. Relax the muscles surrounding your lips, eyes, and forehead. Relax the eyes, the lips, the head, and the muscles.

Spend a little more time in any areas that seem somewhat heavy or murky in their energy (as if the air above that body part is heavier), or if you sense energy elevated in particular areas. Make use of your instincts. Once finished, in gratitude, return your hands to your heart.

Your whole body is now relaxed. From head to toe, all muscles and organs are relaxed. Release yourself into the relaxation of the body and mind.

In this state, quietly repeat, "I have complete confidence in Reiki." Reiki is going to rejuvenate and cure me."

3. Energize

Take a deep breath in through your mouth and out through your nose.

Consider a gorgeous golden luminous ball hovering above your head. Watch it drift down and merge with the Crown Chakra. See the golden violet beams invigorating the nervous system and the right eye as they expand into the various systems.

Say quietly to yourself, "I am divinely protected, led, and at peace."

Imagine the golden ball slowly separating from the Crown Chakra and floating down to join the Brow Chakra. Watch it merge with the lovely indigo wheel of the Brow Chakra. Visualize golden indigo beams energizing the pituitary, hypothalamus, nose, left eye, and ears, and mentally repeat to yourself, "I am open to new ideas, people, and circumstances, and I trust my instincts."

See the golden ball detach from the Brow Chakra and gently float and drop into the Throat Chakra's bright blue wheel. Consider the golden blue rays invigorating the neck, upper lungs, digestive tract, bronchial, and upper stomach regions. Tell yourself, "I feel secure expressing my sentiments." "I adore, trust, and value my creative abilities."

Imagine the golden ball dissolving into the brilliant green wheel of the Heart Chakra. Observe how the golden-green beam enters the thymus, heart, blood, lower lungs, upper liver, and arms. "Love is the meaning of my life," tell yourself. It's all over."

See the golden ball detach and enter the Solar Plexus Chakras, where it will merge with the yellow wheel and disseminate golden yellow rays throughout the digestive system, pancreas, liver, gallbladder, intestines, and spleen. "I believe in my merit," you tell yourself. "I am deserving of the finest in life."

Imagine the golden ball breaking free from the Solar Plexus Chakra and falling down to the Sacral Chakra, to the orange wheel three fingers from the navel. Consider the golden ball mixing with the orange wheel, with golden orange rays passing through the whole reproductive system. Repeat to yourself, "Love is the purpose of my life. It is everywhere."

See the golden ball split and float down to the Root Chakra, which is the seat of Kundalini energy. It may be seen mixing with the red-colored wheel. The bright red rays are stimulating the kidneys, bladder, spine, and lower limbs as they expand throughout the excretory system. Feel the heat. "I am always protected and secure," repeat. I love my feet because they guide me. "I adore my legs because they support me."

Continue to breathe in through your nose and out through your nose. Feel completely at ease. Feel the richness of love pouring through all the centers. All disturbing feelings have vanished. You are serene, at ease, and firmly planted.

Now imagine that you are surrounded by light. Feel your aura growing and being shielded by white light. There is no bad energy that may damage you. You are completely safe.

4. Activate

Using Reiki, activate the 5 elements. Imagine holding the earth in your hands, thanking it, energizing it, and blessing it with Reiki. Imagine water in your hands, praise it, excite it, and bless it with Reiki energy. Now visualize holding the fire in your hands, thanking it, energizing it, and blessing it with Reiki. Imagine the air in your hands, praise it, energize it, and bless it with Reiki energy. Imagine holding the space/sun/stars/moon/planets in your hands, thanking it and energizing it with Reiki energy.

Your Reiki meditation/Gassho has come to an end. Slowly return to the tips of your toes from your head, ears, chest, and legs. Stretch your arms and legs slowly. Gently open your eyes and become aware of your surroundings. You'll feel energized and great in every way.

You are now completely empowered with Reiki. Consider yourself in front of you. Offer yourself Reiki. Heal yourself and your loved ones. Forgive yourself, as well as your family members.

Step 3: The Healing

Okay, now we're ready to perform Reiki self-healing:

1: Begin by softly placing your hands in a prayer posture in the center of your chest, just below your chin. Keep your hands in this posture for a few moments as you concentrate on your in and out breaths. Breathe gently and deeply once more to induce relaxation of your body and mind.

2: Place both hands gently on your head. Take a few deep, relaxing breaths. Focus on your hands on the top of your head. Allow the muscles and skin on your head to relax and heal while you hold this hand posture.

REIKI FOR BEGINNERS

3: Place both hands gently over your jaws. Breathe in deep, calm breaths once more. Focus on your hands over your jaws and allow it to relax and heal.

4: Place the hands gently over the eyes. Avoid putting your hands over your nose for better breathing. Allow the muscles and skin of your forehead, face, and eyes to relax and heal while you hold this hand posture.

5: Place your right hand gently over your throat. Continue to take deep, relaxing breaths. Focus on your throat. Try not to put too much pressure on your neck for your own comfort. Allow the muscles in your neck, throat, and upper chest to relax and heal while you hold this hand posture.

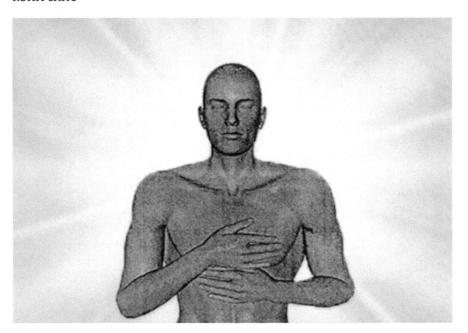

6: Place your right hand on your heart and left hand just below it. Continue to inhale slowly and deeply. Direct your focus on the heart. Allow the muscles in the middle of your chest and ribcage to relax and heal while you hold this hand posture.

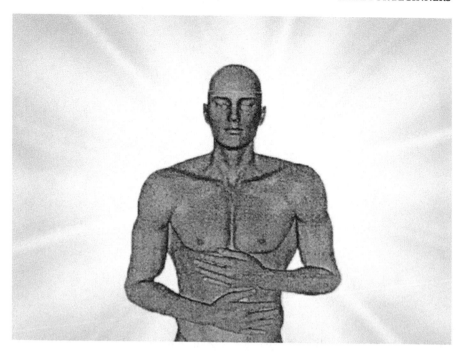

7: Gently place your right hand at the pit of the stomach in front of the aorta, in the Solar Plexus region. Place your left hand just above the right hand. Continue to inhale slowly and deeply. Keep your focus on this part of your body. Allow the muscles in this region to relax and heal by maintaining this hand posture.

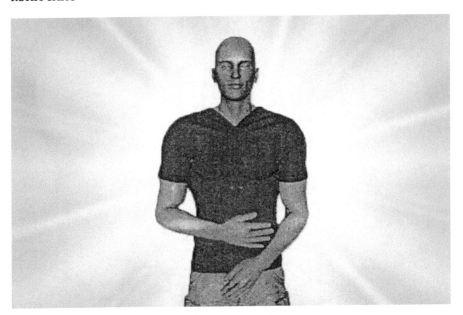

8: Place both your hands on the Sacral Chakra (below the navel, where the perineum is) and Root Chakra respectively, as shown in the figure. Continue to inhale slowly and deeply. Put your focus on this part of your body. Allow the muscles in this region to relax and heal while retaining this hand posture.

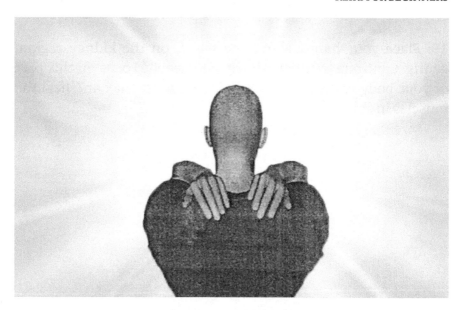

9: Place both hands gently on the shoulder muscles. Continue to inhale slowly and deeply. Focus on this part of your body and allow this hand posture to relax and heal the muscles in this area.

10: Place your hands above the waist, on the kidney region, gently. Continue to inhale slowly and deeply. Focus on this part of your body and allow this hand posture to relax and heal the muscles in this area.

11: Put your hands on either the tops or soles of your feet. To reach, gently bend; don't overwork yourself. Focus on this part of your body and allow this hand posture to relax and heal the muscles in this area.

Step 4: Sealing Off Energy

After completing a healing session, it is critical to express gratitude, cleanse oneself, and seal the energy. It may be as easy as taking a step back, washing your hands clean, and saying a prayer to thank yourself, the energy, and the receiver for the exchange. You may also draw a huge circle, crossing your arms in front of your body to represent the union of your two energies, and finishing with hands in prayer.

Note:

- Try to follow the hand posture instructions in the sequence instructed. However, feel free to make any changes you think would benefit you. Lay your hands on any additional parts of your body that you believe need relaxation and healing.
- It is recommended that you do each hand position for 2 minutes during a 20-minute self-treatment. Some of the hand postures may need you to hold them for

a longer period of time than others. But don't stress about the precise timing. You will learn the hand placements with practice. Also, don't be concerned about doing the hand postures perfectly. Simply surrender and do your best. That will be good enough.

What to Do Before and After Your Reiki Session?

Before the session, perform the following:

1. Unwind and Reflect

Allow at least 30 minutes before the session to sit and contemplate. Check in with your body and make a note of any emotions, thoughts, or physical sensations you are having.

Take some time to breathe and attend to your body's demands on any given day. Before you begin, consider any intensions you want to set for your session, as well as anything you want.

2. Eat and Hydrate

You'll want to make sure you've eaten and hydrated a few hours before the session, mostly so you're not distracted by hunger or thirst.

However, you should avoid eating a large meal before your session since you don't want all of your body's energy to be spent toward digestion when you're having therapy.

3. Make Yourself Comfortable

Comfort is essential if you want to be receptive to receiving and integrating Reiki energy.

Wear garments that are loose and breathable. Because shoes are removed during the session and the feet might get cool, I advise wearing socks.

You should also use the restroom before the session. Also, if the posture you're in during your session is unpleasant in any way, alter it; make sure you're as comfortable as possible.

Following your Reiki session, perform the following:

1. Consolidate

Many of the advantages of Reiki may be felt shortly after the session concludes. As a result, it's critical to locate a calm and soothing place to assimilate whatever may occur. Meditating at least 15-20 minutes after the session, lying down, going for a stroll in nature, or even napping is good.

Avoid planning or scheduling anything shortly after your session.

2. Rehydrate and Eat Again

It is critical to hydrate after doing any sort of energy activity. After your session, consume 1-2 glasses of water. Adding electrolytes to your water is also a good idea since it helps to refresh the body.

Energy work is typically hungry work, and you may feel hungry right after your session as well. Make sure to listen to your body and follow up with a nutritious snack or meal if necessary. Eating may also assist in centering the body, and as an added benefit, something sweet may taste exceptionally nice after a session of energy training.

3. Contemplate

It's helpful to spend some time reflecting after the session, whether by writing, painting, or otherwise recording any insights you had throughout the experience.

You may also choose to meditate or listen to relaxing and/or motivating music afterward. Find an activity that helps you connect to what you've encountered so you may count on it in the future.

REIKI SYMBOLS FOR DISTANCE HEALING

Using symbols is a powerful approach to Reiki distance healing. It is one of the most vital and intriguing aspects of Reiki. Reiki symbols enable the practitioner to direct the flow of universal life force energy to achieve specific outcomes. It's how you improve your Reiki practice.

Although Reiki symbols are typically meant to be kept a secret, they've gained a lot of attention and noise over the years. They assist individuals to take their Reiki practice to the next level by enabling them to channel Reiki energy for a particular goal. Unlike other symbols, which just impact the subconscious, Reiki symbols actively alert the mind and body to modify the way the Reiki energy operates.

They are a great, lovely way to connect with a higher power. Their usage does not need the ability to meditate or years of spiritual practice. Their power and efficacy are given to us by grace, allowing us to embrace the worth we get as a gift from the Creator with humility. They are energized by the practitioner's goal of focus. We should be thankful for Dr. Usui's efforts, as well as the efforts of all others who have worked tirelessly to make this healing system known to us.

The 5 Reiki symbols listed below are regarded as the most precious. Each may be identified by its Japanese name or by its intention, a symbolic term that expresses its goals in practice.

Simply envision the person to whom you are sending energy and then create the symbol in the air with your hand while seeing the symbol in your mind's eye. The symbols bring strength and purpose to your energy transfer. There are many symbols for different reasons, therefore when you apply the Reiki symbols, your energy transfer may become highly concentrated and specific. You can make it happen as long as you use intention in the activation process.

Things to Know about Reiki Symbols

Before we proceed, a few points should be addressed.

1. When it comes to Reiki, you should understand that all symbols are equally beneficial. There is no greater sign than the other. It all relies on your requirements and intentions. Reiki symbols may have a variety of vibrations. As a result, they may be employed in a variety of ways.

2. Reiki symbols will not make you a better practitioner. Using hand positions as the only way you do Reiki can be enough to find the results you're looking for. You should never disregard this technique.

3. Reiki symbols are a fascinating subject, and I can see why they are so popular. Just be cautious not to let them become the focal point of your practice. Consider using them just as a means of increasing your awareness and consciousness towards spiritual growth. The true work you need to do is with your inner self.

How to Use Reiki Symbols?

They may be activated by drawing in the air with one's hand, imagining them in one's thoughts, repeating their names aloud or to oneself, or just thinking about them. They are triggered automatically for certain advanced practitioners whenever they are required during a session.

They may seem complex to draw at first—especially the 3rd one with its numerous strokes—but you'll be glad to know that there is no wrong way to draw them. Symbols are drawn differently by different masters. The variances in the symbols do not affect their usefulness. There is no correct or incorrect way to draw the symbols. What matters is the practitioner's purpose while invoking them.

Invoking the symbols

Draw the symbol in the direction you want to transfer Reiki energy using your dominant hand's index finger. Chant (or quietly summon) the symbol's mantra 3 times. For example, if you're preparing to perform Reiki healing on someone, draw the power symbol over them and say the mantra 3 times.

Try to make the symbol the right size. For example, if you're using the Reiki power sign to create a protective shield for a building, room, or other items, picture drawing the symbol to cover the entire space. But don't worry if you make a mistake; just try your best.

Remember, your intention is the most crucial thing.

Types of Reiki Symbols

Reiki symbols are classified into several degrees and systems. Each Reiki level and system represents a spiritual threshold that must be crossed to attain an efficient condition of healing, awareness, and higher consciousness. As a result, the intensity and vibration of the symbols might vary.

There are symbols for:

- Balancing and harmonizing
- Mental and emotional recovery
- Adding a dimension to a specific location or region
- Healing and unblocking emotional and communication stumbling blocks

- Encircling and filling oneself with energy
- Communicating with certain angels/archangels
- Restoring balance to your energy fields and energy centers (chakras)
- Balancing your chakras
- Grounding
- Abundance

Cho Ku Rei: The Symbol of Power

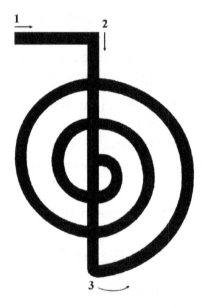

If you're wanting to either boost or reduce power, Cho Ku Rei is the sign for you. It is represented by a depiction of a coil (drawn clockwise or counterclockwise) and signifies Chi. Consider the power symbol to be a "switch," so once triggered, the Reiki practitioner has an increased capacity to illuminate, enlighten, and channel energy in their body.

How to Use Cho Ku Rei

Cho Ku Rei is most commonly used at the start of a Reiki session to assist raise Reiki power at any moment throughout the session. When you're trying to recover from an injury, Cho Ku Rei may assist with anything from minor aches and pains to more significant, excruciating ailments.

In a broader sense, Cho Ku Rei might be used when you're attempting to eliminate bad energy that may have been lodged during your Reiki session. And, if you wish to incorporate Cho Ku Rei's negative energy-clearing ability into your daily life, consider sketching the sign on the walls of spaces where you want the energy to be bright and positive.

Cho Ku Rei may also be used to revitalize your relationships. It may also defend against misfortunes, which are usually caused by impure energy, therefore activating Cho Ku Rei is a great approach to cleanse the energy systems.

Sei He Ki: The Symbol of Harmony

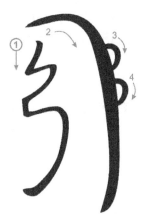

Turn to Sei He Ki, the harmony symbol, when you require cleansing and mental and emotional equilibrium. The main meaning of Sei He Ki is "God and man become one," and the picture for Sei He Ki resembles either a cresting wave about to fall over a beach or a bird's wing. It may also help to balance the right and left parts of the brain and is often seen as a Reiki protection symbol in addition to being a harmony symbol.

How to Use Sei He Ki:

If you want to learn something new, ace an exam, or just boost your memory in general? Sei He Ki can assist you.

Additionally, if you're having trouble breaking a negative habit—such as excessive drinking, smoking, or overeating, try calling on Sei He Ki for assistance. Harmful habits and addictions are often the results of terrible experiences or negative views about yourself, and seeing the Sei He Ki symbol around you may help you create a more positive picture of yourself, so assisting in the elimination of these bad habits.

Many headaches are caused by mental and emotional instability, and using Sei He Ki to balance this out may help eliminate headaches (and the need for artificial pain relievers!). It also shields you against bad energies in general, functioning as a protective sign that may both protect you from negativity and expel negativity from the body. Even better, Sei He Ki may strengthen your affirmations. If you write your affirmations down, consider drawing the Sei He Ki symbol next to them—they'll be far more likely to stay.

Hon Sha Ze Sho Nen: The Symbol of Distance

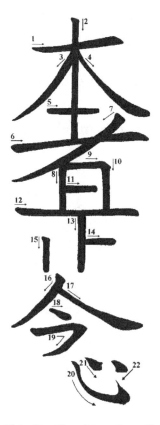

The concept of Hon Sha Ze Sho Nen is a little harder to understand than some of the other Reiki symbols, but not by much. The term Hon Sha Ze Sho Nen means "no present, past, or future," and it is used to convey Reiki energy over time and space. Although Hon Sha Ze Sho Nen cannot erase the past, it may help heal old wounds by reframing the situation and making it into a learning experience rather than merely a traumatic occurrence with no rhyme or reason. Hon Sha Ze Sho Nen may also assist Reiki practitioners in sending Reiki into the future, before events such as assessments, doctor's visits, or unpleasant conversations with loved ones.

How to Use Hon Sha Ze Sho Nen:

While Hon Sha Ze Sho Nen is regarded as one of the most powerful symbols, it must be applied appropriately for it to be effective. The distance Reiki symbol is more powerful when used on the subtle body rather than the physical body, and Reiki experts recommend that this symbol be employed daily to successfully facilitate past and future healing in the body.

Dai Ko Myo: The Master Symbol

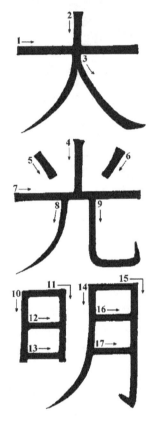

All praise the mighty Dai Ko Myo, or master symbol. This is the holiest Reiki symbol, and it is both nourishing and illuminating. It has the highest vibration and the greatest transformational potential of the 5 Reiki symbols. Dai Ko Myo's healing qualities are all-encompassing, curing the higher chakras, the aura, and the soul as a whole. Dai Ko Myo means "great enlightenment" or "bright dazzling light." It brings Reiki practitioners closer to God by assisting in the path of spiritual enlightenment.

How to Use Dai Ko Myo:

To invoke Dai Ko Myo, you may employ a variety of techniques, including drawing the sign (a series of characters), picturing it, or drawing it with your Third Eye. You may also meditate with the Dai Ko Myo symbol to receive it, which will feed your body and soul and give you the strength to assist yourself before going out into the world to serve others.

If you're focusing on improving your connection with yourself, gaining greater self-awareness, or developing a better spiritual practice, Dai Ko Myo is a crucial symbol to invoke, and employing it in conjunction with other Reiki symbols only makes it more potent.

Dai Ko Myo is also a fantastic approach to help boost your immune system since it enhances the flow of energy throughout the whole body, which may help eliminate blockages that may be preventing your immune system from functioning properly. Furthermore, if you're employing homeopathic medicines to treat your health or improve your life (for example, herbal tinctures or essential oils), Dai Ko Myo may assist boost their effectiveness. It is also useful for charging and clearing crystals.

Raku: The symbol of Completion

Raku is a Reiki symbol used at the master level, and it's also known as the "fire serpent"—and its form explains why. It's a zig-zag, lightning-bolt-like form that's mostly used for grounding after Reiki. Raku, which is drawn from head to ground, is used to let the body accept the benefits of Reiki, much as savasana is used at the end of yoga to help the body absorb all the benefits of the practice. Above all, Raku is a grounding symbol, and Reiki practitioners should use it to eliminate any bad energy they may have acquired from the person they were practicing on.

How to Use Raku:

Use it at the end of a Reiki practice to ground and receive all the benefits of the energy transfer. And if you ever need a moment of grounding in your daily life, feel free to draw the symbol to experience the advantages of grounding.

How to Use Multiple Reiki Symbols at Once?

Reiki symbols do not have to be used individually; they may even be used in combination. One way to do this is to use multiple symbols to help send Reiki. Begin by holding an image of a person and repeating or drawing the symbols Cho Ku Rei, Sei Hei Ki, Sei He Ki, Hon Sha Ze Sho Nen 3 times each. Then, while holding the recipient's image, pronounce his or her name 3 times. This is an excellent approach to provide them with healing energy.

Another fantastic approach to employ many symbols at once is to send Reiki to a future event that makes you worried or may bring negative news—such as a job interview, a doctor's visit, and so on. Say the symbols Cho Ku Rei, Sei Hei Ki, Sei He Ki, Hon Sha Ze Sho Nen 3 times each, and imagine them while requesting them to offer you serenity and soothing vibes on the day of the event. As a result, by the time the event you're expecting arrives, you'll be less worried and better able to concentrate on what's going on around you.

While employing these symbols is a fantastic method to enhance your physical, mental, emotional, and spiritual well-being, it's okay to just focus on hand postures during your initial Reiki sessions. After you've had a few sessions of Reiki and gained some experience, you'll have a deeper understanding of each of these symbols and how to use them in your daily life.

HEALING OTHERS

You may heal others too after you've reached a certain point in your Reiki practice. As an intermediate, you must be close to the patient seeking healing. As you progress and become assured that you can provide hands-on healing, you can provide distance healing to anybody, anywhere in the world, besides hands-on healing.

Hands-on Healing (Reiki Level 1)

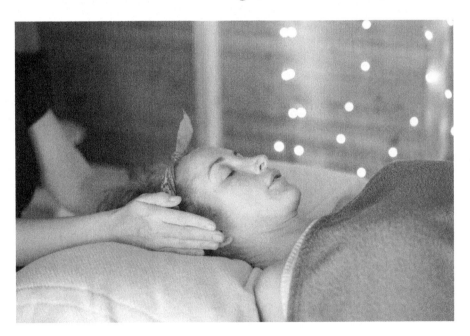

1. If you want to offer someone Reiki Hands-on healing, ask them to wear comfortable, loose-fitting clothing. When they ar-

rive for the healing, ask them to take off their glasses, watch, jewelry, belt, and so on. It is allowed to wear gold and silver jewelry. Make sure that both you and the patient consume a glass of water.

2. Before you send Reiki, ask them to allow the Reiki energy to heal and treat all of their levels of being. Allow them to accept this healing energy.

3. Next, instruct them to sit or lie down with their eyes closed. Making them lay down is the most convenient option for both the healer and the patient, since the healer has easy access to all chakras and the patient may totally rest.

4. Place yourself next to the recipient's head. Consider directing a constant stream of healing light from your hands into the back of their head (Crown Chakra).

5. Ask them to take multiple rounds of deep breaths while carefully counting a 3-second inhalation and a 3-5 second exhale.

6. Visualize the healing light as it enters their body and slowly and softly fills them up. Visualize all of their bodily organs and parts bathed in Reiki energy. Consider them to be alight with healing energy. See them expanded and their initial energy layer has been filled. The energy then emanates from their physical body.

7. Then transmit Reiki to their emotional being. Consider them to be filled with peace, joy, love, satisfaction, and general well-being. Consider how the radiance of their physical body has now spread to their emotional level.

8. Next, transmit Reiki to their mental being. Assume that their thoughts are clear and peaceful. Imagine that their brain is operating such that thoughts flow effortlessly and are well thought out. Imagine that answers to puzzling situations come readily. Consider how anxiety gradually drains out of their body. As all of their unpleasant thoughts leave their body, Reiki fills up and spreads to their mental level.

9. Then transmit Reiki to their spiritual being. Imagine Reiki entering and filling and restoring their spirit—their essence—their soul. Consider it a lovely golden flow of energy that provides a direct conduit to the higher worlds. Assume that guidance is flowing in and that they are linking to the source, whatever that source may be. Intend that the Reiki energy reconnects them to the divine inside them and rekindles their spark. Consider them to be infused with the spiritual energy that reaches beyond all other levels of their existence.

10. You may also accomplish this by communicating with the individual before delivering Reiki. You may address each level of being before the session by asking questions—how they are feeling bodily, mentally, or emotionally? Are they in any discomfort or pain?

11. For the emotional body, you might inquire as to how they are feeling emotionally. Is there anything making them happy or sad?

12. Then inquire whether they have too much on their thoughts or are concerned about anything. Is their head feel like it is ready to explode?

13. To address the spiritual dimension, ask as to how their soul is feeling. Do they sense the holiness of everyday life, or is it simply another day? Do they feel alone and unprotected in the world?

14. For 10-20 minutes, send Reiki to each level of being, intending for the Reiki to go to the concerns, thoughts, or emotions that you addressed. Visualize the body getting healed, relaxed, and heavy in preparation for a restful night's sleep. You may provide Reiki for as long as you wish, but 10-20 minutes is generally enough to leave them feeling calm and tranquil.

15. Allow them to relax after the session is over. Visualize a power symbol over them and close the session with light and love. Awaken the patient gently. Then express gratitude for the

gift of Reiki.

16. Do dry bathing (Kenyoku) or seal off the energy to separate from their energy field. You may contact them afterward to find out what they experienced and to share what you felt.

Distant Healing (Reiki Level 2)

Channels attuned to Reiki 2 or above may do distant healing. When providing distance healing to someone, it is preferable to ask them to set aside some time to receive the energy you provide them. This boosts their ability to absorb energy and their drive to heal themselves. Ask them to sit with their eyes closed, bare feet on the floor, and no hands or legs crossed. Ask them to sense and accept the energy that is coming to them.

There are various methods for transmitting distant energy. You may use an item as a surrogate—such as a picture or an intention slip—or you could envision them or transmit Reiki via your Third Eye. Each of these principles is thoroughly discussed below.

Techniques of Distant Healing:

Using a Photograph

Having a picture of the person receiving the energy transfer is a useful tool when giving Reiki. Looking at someone's picture may help you direct the energy you're giving to that individual more precisely. While it is easy to see this person in your mind, it is usually more compelling to gaze at them in a photograph. By glancing at the picture, you will see and connect with their energy on a subconscious level. Then imagine sending Reiki to them, which will surround them in glorious light.

Draw the symbols on the back of the photograph, and if there is enough room, you might even write that their issue has been solved above it. While providing Reiki, hold the photo between your hands and envision the symbols on it.

Using Reiki Symbols

Using the symbols taught in level II Reiki training is an effective form of Reiki distance healing. You would picture the person to whom you are giving energy and then draw the symbol in the air with your hand while seeing the symbol in your mind's eye. The symbols bring strength and purpose to your energy transfer. There are different symbols for different purposes, therefore when you apply the Reiki symbols, your energy transfer may become highly concentrated and specialized.

Using the Recipient's Name

One efficient way to transfer Reiki energy is to put down the name of the person to whom you want to send the Reiki. You may also draw the Reiki symbol you want to use below their name. Fold the paper in half and hold it in your hands. Visualize yourself transmitting healing energy from your hands into the paper, and hence to your subject.

Using a Surrogate

If you want to use your hands for Reiki healing rather than visualization, you might use a stuffed animal or another comparable item as a surrogate. Believe the toy to be the patient and begin administering it Reiki. Then, using your hands, draw the Reiki symbols over the thing and lay your hands on it to transmit the energy. As though you were doing an in-person healing session, you may employ the particular hand positions on the item.

Using Your Imagination

Keep your hands cupped together and visualize the person, either within your palms or in front of you, receiving and soaking in the energy you transmit. Imagine them feeling better and draw the symbols as you give them Reiki.

Using the Third Eye

If the individual is visible, visualize Reiki energy entering your Third Eye and flowing to that person. Imagine a Reiki ray flowing out of your Third Eye and use that beam to draw the symbols on them. You might perform this method while staring at their portrait or just envisioning them standing in front of you and getting Reiki via your Third Eye.

Making Use of Intention Slip

You could have an intention box that fits in your hand and contains rolled-up papers. On one side of a little chit of paper, write your intention. Use only positive words (avoid saying 'no,' 'not,' 'don't,' 'won't,' 'can't,' etc.), avoid any full stops (period.), and don't fold the page. Finish with 'It is so, thank you Reiki, Thy will be done' after the intention. Draw all the symbols on the other side of the page. Put it in the intention box after rolling it up.

The intention box has the benefit of allowing you to deliver Reiki to numerous people/events at the same time. Hold the box between your hands whenever you want, mentally draw the symbols on it, and offer Reiki. You don't have to address all intentions individually.

A Word on Adults vs. Kids

If you're giving Reiki to your mate or other adults, keep in mind that some people may have lost how to feel (or have grown less conscious of) their energy and physical bodies over time. That's OK. Just be aware that they may say that they cannot feel the energy flowing. It may be slight, but it does not imply that your energy did not have an effect on them.

When dealing with children, depending on their age, it might also be beneficial to explain what you are doing and why. Children are very observant and receptive to alternate techniques. Some parents may also teach their children how to accept energy and practice Reiki so that they can access their doorway to healing at a young age.

HEALING WITH CRYSTALS

Crystals are marketed as ancient forms of healing, with ideologies derived from Hinduism and Buddhism. It is crucial to note, however, that there is no scientific evidence to support the usage of crystals. People are nonetheless captivated by their hues and attractiveness, despite this.

Crystal healing is a complementary medicine approach in which crystals and other stones are used to treat illnesses and prevent disease. Supporters of this practice claim that crystals work as therapeutic conduits, enabling good, healing energy to enter the body while bad, disease-causing energy exits.

When crystal healing is paired with Reiki, it's like turning on the healing turbo! Crystals contain their own natural energy. They put everything back into equilibrium and hasten the body's natural healing process.

They are becoming popular in the Reiki world because they can aid in deeper healing. They may help us mend the chakras and balance the energy system by eliminating the energy blocks. Plus, crystals may assist us in channeling deeper and quicker healing. They are a suggested tool for all Reiki practitioners, and working with them can be a lot of fun.

You don't have to do anything other than putting a crystal in your surroundings for it to operate. However, if you do add your intent and energy, your crystals will perform better since they will take up on your intention and multiply it manyfold. And if Reiki is the energy that flows through you, your crystals will absorb it, magnify its influence, and concentrate it.

There are various kinds of crystals that have unique healing qualities for the mind, body, and soul. They are said to increase the flow of positive energy and aid in the removal of bad energy from the body and psyche for physical and emotional benefits.

You may charge a crystal with Reiki energy and take it with you or give it to someone who needs it. The intricate and effective crystals dissolve blocked and stagnant energy, remove negative energy—such as stress—from the body, and boost the body's natural self-healing for a variety of common health conditions.

Each crystal is organized into color groupings and has therapeutic and metaphysical characteristics, chakra linkages, and Reiki symbol links. Three of the most frequently used crystals by Reiki masters are Quartz, Amethyst, and Citrine.

How to Activate Any Crystal?

Reiki crystals are quite easy to use. Some practitioners just wash the crystals and put them on certain regions of the body while doing the Reiki therapy. This is known as "crystal programming," and it is a highly valuable addition to Reiki healings because it acts as an additional pair of healing hands.

When concentrating on chakra balancing, we should match the hues of the crystals to the colors of the chakras. Having said that, we'd go for Amethyst for the Third Eye Chakra and Clear Quartz for the Crown Chakra.

Of all, this is only the beginning of Reiki healing with crystals, and it isn't the only method to choose Reiki crystals. Rose Quartz, for example, is a pink healing stone that is often used for the Heart Chakra. So besides matching the chakra colors, it's crucial to apply common sense.

Simply perform the following to activate a crystal:

1. First, choose the healing stone with the attributes that are most suitable for the underlying issue you are at-

tempting to heal.
2. Hold it in your palm.
3. Cleanse it with Reiki energy using intention and symbols.
4. Concentrate on your healing goal and communicate it to the crystal.
5. Finally, just let the energy flow between your hands and through the crystal. This may continue for anywhere between 5-15 minutes, or until you feel the energy begin to cool.
6. The healing crystal is then placed on the targeted body area, and your hands are placed over it to channel Reiki.

Different Types of Healing Crystals

Clear Quartz

This white crystal is referred to as a "master healer." It is supposed to boost energy by absorbing, storing, releasing, and regulating it. It's also said to help with focus and memory. Clear crystals are said to help activate the immune system and regulate the overall body. This stone is often combined with others—such as rose quartz—to help and improve its properties.

Smoky Quartz

It is a brownish grey, transparent form of quartz that varies in clarity from almost full transparency to an almost opaque brownish-gray or black crystal. Smoky quartz is said to aid in general well-being, the removal of undesirable emotional baggage, the surrender of old wounds, stability, and grounding.

It is said to bring us closer to the Earth. It is the stone we choose as our overall good luck stone, since it may offer us luck in a variety of ways. The primary reason for this is because it cleanses your energy field of bad energy while attracting good energy.

Rose Quartz

This pink stone is all about love, as the color suggests. It is supposed to help re-establish trust and harmony in all types of relationships while also increasing their intimate bonds. It's also said to provide peace and tranquillity through times of loss.

But it's not all about other people. Rose quartz is also known to promote self-love, respect, trust, and value, which is something we could all use in this day and age.

Jasper

This shining crystal is renowned as the "ultimate nurturer." It is claimed to energize the soul and help you through stressful situations by preparing you to completely "show up." It is said to shield you from bad energy and absorb it, while also fostering bravery, fast-thinking, and confidence. These are qualities that are very useful when dealing with difficult circumstances, precisely what this stone may be useful for.

Obsidian

Obsidian, a fiercely defensive stone, is thought to assist in the formation of a barrier against the physical and mental negative. It is also supposed to assist in the removal of emotional blockages and to enhance attributes of strength, clarity, and compassion to aid in the discovery of one's real sense of self. It may assist with digestion and cleansing, as well as perhaps reducing discomfort and cramping in your physical body.

Carnelian

This is a success-boosting stone and one of the luckiest good luck charms known to mankind. It represents bold energy, warmth, and a delight that lasts as long as it empowers and stimulates. It is regarded as a stone representing bravery, endurance, vitality, leadership, and drive. Carnelians' vibrant, rich hue has inspired and safeguarded humanity throughout history. This crystal not only looks lovely, but it also instills confidence, vitality, and creativity in those who use it.

Citrine

Citrine can bring excitement, curiosity, and passion to all aspects of your life. It is claimed to help you shed undesirable tendencies from your life (like fear) and to promote optimism, warmth, motivation, and clarity. It is also said to improve mindful traits—such as creativity and focus.

Turquoise

This blue crystal is supposed to provide healing properties for the mind, body, and soul. In general, it is regarded as a good luck charm that may assist you in balancing your emotions while seeking spiritual grounding. It is supposed to assist the respiratory, skeletal, and immunological systems of the body.

Aquamarine

The color aquamarine is connected with trust and letting go.

Aquamarine was formerly thought to be the treasure of mermaids. Sailors used the stone as a charm to bring them good fortune on the open seas. The stone was also used as a sign of protection and bravery.

Aquamarine harnesses Water energy, which is associated with serenity, peaceful power, and cleansing. It represents untapped potential. It is yielding, formless, and forceful, all at the same time. The Water element can regenerate and revive.

The Tiger's Eye

This golden stone may be for you if you need a burst of power or inspiration. It is supposed to assist in the removal of fear, worry, and self-doubt from the mind and body. This might be good for job goals or even for personal concerns. Tiger's Eye is also claimed to assist in the attainment of harmony and balance, allowing you to make clear, mindful judgments.

Amethyst

This purple crystal is said to be extremely protecting, healing, and purifying. It helps clear the mind of negative thoughts and brings out humility, honesty, and spiritual insight. It is also supposed to assist in the promotion of sobriety.

Another purported advantage of this stone is that it helps with sleep, from insomnia treatment to dream analysis. It is supposed to increase hormone production, cleanse the blood, and reduce pain and tension.

Moonstone

Moonstone, which is associated with "fresh beginnings," is supposed to promote inner growth and power. When beginning afresh, this crystal is said to calm those unsettling sensations of tension and instability, allowing you to go ahead effectively. It is also said to enhance positive thinking, intuition, and inspiration, as well as prosperity and good fortune.

TIPS TO BOOST YOUR REIKI GROWTH

Some practices can boost your Reiki growth. These catalyze Reiki healing along with providing their own benefits. Here are 3 practices you can use to take your Reiki practice a notch higher:

Yoga

Power is calculated in numbers. Magic may be created by two individuals who work effectively together. Similarly, I've discovered that combining two healing skills may significantly boost their respective strengths. Especially when combining Yoga with Reiki.

Yoga, like Reiki, may be performed with little to no equipment and its postures can be modified to various degrees of mobility. It has profound emotional and spiritual impacts besides its physical advantages.

You'll get a lot out of combining Reiki and Yoga since they're both accessible and adaptable, and they have the same meditative healing properties. Both are forms of energy therapy that will help you deepen and amplify your experience.

Reiki and yoga complement each other. They may be used in concert with one another to achieve major transformation. Yoga is like peeling back the layers of an onion. As each layer peels away, more and more of the self is revealed. The process may be both powerful and frightening.

A slow-paced, gentle yoga class—such as Yin Yoga—is ideal for combining with Reiki. The long holds of Yin Yoga ground postures allow a Reiki practitioner to spend time with oneself in the quiet of your body and mind.

Healing Preparation

1. To get set to heal with both yoga and Reiki, replace your uncertainty and fear with a spirit of adventure!
2. Before initiating asana, begin with calm, purposeful breathing and meditation. Your asana practice might range from a few minutes to an entire yoga session. After movement, choose a supported seat or reclining posture like Savasana to begin Reiki self-treatment.
3. Have an open heart and let go of any attachment to the result of your session. Even though Reiki and Yoga are completely different, combining them might be a fortuitous finding for nurturing the inner self.

Pranayamas (Breathing Exercises)

Pranayama, or breathing exercises, is a well-known component of yoga. Pranayama is a set of traditional Indian breathing techniques. Prana is a Sanskrit word that signifies "breathe," "spirit," "life-force," "vitality," "vigor," and "energy."

The exercises include the art of experimenting with retentions of breath, inhalations, and exhalations to create energy, balance, and relaxation. For Reiki, pranayama, among other things, may assist channel Reiki. There are several pranayama techniques to choose from.

The following are some of the reasons pranayama is helpful when combined with Reiki practice:

1. It Allows Us to Be Aware of and Release Our Resistance

Pranayama teaches us to recognize where we retain tension in our body and then choose to breathe through it. We can make more room in our hearts, shoulders, and other regions where we used to keep tough emotions over time. The greater the amount of space we make, the more life-force energy we may call in and channel.

2. Helps Get Rid of the Unnecessary

We exchange emotions, perspectives, energy, and thoughts that don't benefit us when we intentionally move the breath through us. Pranayama assists in the release and transmutation of the old from our beings to make room for Reiki.

3. Promotes Health

Digestion and elimination are aided by diaphragmatic breathing. It maintains a healthy level of breathing, heart rate, and immunological function. We cannot perform our dharma to the fullest extent unless we are comfortable in our physical bodies. Pranayama generates life and energy, allowing us to serve and share Reiki.

4. Improves Intuition

Alternate nostril breathing unites the two hemispheres of the brain, allowing us to balance our rational and analytical minds while also tapping into our intuitive side. Using these activities before meditation relaxes yet alerts my mind, allowing me to lean in to hear what my soul has to say.

5. Oxygenates Our Cells

We are more responsive to Qi/Prana and Reiki when we are well oxygenated.

6. Strengthens the Nervous System

Pranayama stimulates the flow of blood to the brain and endocrine glands. It causes the parasympathetic nervous system and the relaxation response to be activated. We are better able to surrender and let Reiki flow through us when we allow for a relaxation response.

7. Enhances Concentration

Pranayama assists us in entering a contemplative state, which is necessary for Reiki to flow through us.

"Breath is the link that connects life to consciousness, and it connects your body to your thoughts. Whenever your mind wanders, use your breath as a tool to reclaim control."—Thich Nhat Hanh

8. Teaches Us to Escape Our Egos

Pranayama teaches us how to see the Vrittis and ego and become observers of the mind. Similarly, being a witness to Reiki and realizing that we are a conduit for this energy is beneficial. We have no control over it or the healing it produces, just as we have no control over the Vrittis or the ego.

9. Grounds Us

Ujjayi pranayama is a particular pranayama that is extremely grounding. It is used as an anchor to assist us in returning to the present moment.

10. Brings the Subtle Body in Balance

We reorganize our subtle bodies when we work with our breath. Our chakras align and our nadis clear, resulting in a more powerful auric field.

11. Brings Self-Awareness

We learn about our actual nature by observing our breath. We find our boundless potential and can connect with our Highest Self.

Visualization

Visualization (also known as guided imagery or creative visualization) is a method that involves concentrating your mind on actions or events that you want to happen in your life.

The practice is founded on the concept that your body and mind are inextricably linked. Proponents of visualization claim that presenting positive images, creative imagery, and self-suggestion may change emotions, which then have a physical effect on the body. There are various types of visualizations. Whatever visualization approach you choose, the most important thing is to have a strong intention.

Visualization promotes healing. Just avoid focusing on too many strategies or complicating your recovery by employing too many symbols or affirmations. These are all important practices, but as you get more focused on techniques, your intention begins to wane. Keep it simple, use one strategy to heal one goal, and it will work effectively.

Visualizing Reiki energy flowing through every cell in your body is a great place to start. Feel it engulfing you. Feel the Reiki energy coming into the room and then the house you are in as you continue to breathe. Feel the Reiki energy strengthen as it spreads outdoors onto the land and further into the neighborhood. See it covering your neighborhood, then the country, then the whole world, and eventually the entire universe.

The Visualization Technique:

1. Sit calmly with your eyes closed, breathing freely in and out.
2. When you're ready, concentrate your attention in your mind's eye on the concerned chakra color whirling in front of you. The hue shifts and darkens before lightning again.
3. Pay attention to this color.
4. Breathe in firmly via your nostrils, feeling your abdominals expand as air enters your lungs.
5. As the air enters your body, see it as a chakra color. Hold your breath for a few seconds, then exhale, letting the chakra air evaporate.
6. Continue this regular cycle of inhaling and exhaling while concentrating on your breathing and the color.

Some Other Practices that Can Help Your Reiki Practice

1. Establish a Retreat

Make a specific room in your house for your Reiki practice—a refuge to which you may return each day.

2. Find a Strong, Steady Posture

I start my daily self-practice by selecting a comfortable position that will help my body and mind relax. I usually sit cross-legged on a meditation cushion or lie down to practice. If you're sitting cross-legged, make sure your hips are higher than your knees. If you're laying down, use bolsters to support your knees and neck. You may alternatively sit on a chair with your feet flat on the ground. Experiment with different postures until you discover one that is both engaging and relaxing.

3. Develop a Daily Energy Practice

This might be anything that assists you in tuning into your energy state and achieving equilibrium. You may, for example, begin a regular meditation practice or read inspiring books. Spending more time in nature—whether in the woods or on the beach—is another effective approach to connect with healing energy. Because it vibrates at a high frequency, salt air is a natural energy cleanser.

4. Accept Divine Love

Divine Love is the most potent healing energy at your disposal. Your body remains completely fuelled when you employ Divine Love. All you have to do is embrace the Divine Love energy that is coursing through you. You do this by setting your intention and surrendering to the process. Say, "I embrace Divine Love," with your hands and feet uncrossed and flat on the floor. Take a deep breath in, hold it for 4 seconds, and then exhale through your nose. This will link you.

Remove yourself from the turmoil. Pay attention to what is right in front of you. Whatever you are dealing with, that is what you need to heal. Don't get side-tracked by what's going on halfway across the globe. And don't allow distractions to lure you back into your old habits. Stop watching the news—or TV completely —if necessary. You may also wish to avoid people whose energy does not align with yours. Seek out those who share your beliefs, since they will most likely resonate at a higher frequency.

5. Make Use of Floral Essences

Flower essences are energy and vibrational medicines obtained from live flowers. They may help you move and alter your vibration without causing any harm. When you take a flower essence internally, your essence harmonizes with the flower essence. As a result, they may help you change your focus toward self-love and acceptance.

6. Bathe with Epsom Salts

An Epsom salt bath not only soothes aching muscles but may also alter your energy. Make this a daily routine if possible. Light a candle, play soothing music, and soak for 20 minutes. Pull the drain plug after you're finished, but stay in the bath while the water drains. Visualize all your bad energy and emotions draining away. When you get out of the bath, pat yourself dry gently. Then, either lie down for 10 minutes or go to sleep.

7. Say Affirmations Aloud

How do you think is your energy affected? Your energy will be hindered if you think, "I'm weary," or "I can't do this." Optimistic affirmations have a cascading effect; they may boost your mentality, which helps you feel more positive, which raises your vibration. Try concentrating your thoughts on energizing thoughts. Say aloud a sentence that means something to you, such as "Divine love and positive energies are pouring through me." "I feel more invigorated when I breathe," for example. Assume this is how you feel, and over time, you will.

8. Try Smudging

Smudging is an ancient practice in which sage is burned to cleanse your aura and bless a person or physical space. You just need a smudging wand (usually a thick bunch of white sage). Hold it in your non-dominant hand, light it, and watch the smoke ascend to clear your aura. Breathe in the smoke's aroma and concentrate on yourself and your intention. Then, from the bottom to the top of your head, waft the smoke up and down your body. Finally, place the wand in front of your heart and watch the holy smoke come up. Breathe and repeat any affirmations or visualizations for your personal well-being and spiritual purpose.

9. Make Use of Crystals

All crystals have therapeutic characteristics and may help to improve your energy field. The process of selecting crystals does not have to be difficult. Follow your instincts and do what seems right for you.

I'll discuss crystal in depth ahead in the book...

10. Opt for Journaling

While journaling is not an energy exercise, the written word has a lot of power and may help you become more self-aware, since you can be absolutely honest. When you get up each morning, jot down your plans for the day. Then, at the end of the day, make a list of what you learned.

It will enable you to comprehend the sensory sensations, thoughts, and emotions that may come while meditation. Every day, you can observe how your practice has grown and how it has benefited you.

11. Play Soothing Music

Music at a frequency of 432 Hz resonates with Earth's inherent electromagnetic frequency, which is known as the Schumann Resonance. The Schumann Resonance vibrates at a frequency of 8 Hz on average, which is towards the peak of the Theta brainwave state, when we feel relaxed but still conscious.

When music is made at 432 Hz, a C note is produced at 256 Hz. At precisely 8 Hz, the sympathetic resonances of the note overtones form another C note. When you consider all the artificial electromagnetic frequencies that enter your brainwaves daily—such as those from cell phones, microwaves, and increasingly higher levels of 5G radiation—it makes sense that music tuned to a natural frequency of 432 Hz (8 Hz) would help us feel more balanced. I like to tune in to some soothing music while driving or doing regular chores.

13. Put the 5 Reiki Principles into Action

To support and benefit your life and the lives of others around you, tune into higher vibrations of appreciation and compassion. Integrate the principles of Reiki into your everyday life and meditation practice. Chant or acknowledge them silently:

1. Just for Today, I Release Angry Thoughts
2. Just for Today, I Release Thoughts of Worry
3. Just for Today, I'm Grateful
4. Just for Today, I Expand My Consciousness

15. Express Gratitude

Gratitude is a vibration of divine light. It is a component of the life energy of everything in the physical cosmos. We are in the flow of creation when we live in gratitude, and we enhance the divine light inside ourselves and in the world around us. I don't always know what to do about the world's darkness, but I know that light always illuminates the dark, and that the most powerful tool I have to affect change in the world is to contribute light to the light.

Even in the middle of chaos, gratitude may help us repair our negative thoughts and reach our grateful hearts. It has the potential to strengthen us and make it simpler for us to notice and choose appreciation, wisdom, and love daily. Reiki may help us mend the areas of our lives where we feel stuck and resentful.

You can express gratitude like, 'I'd want to use this opportunity in my practice to thank my guides, the Reiki energy, and myself for co-creating the process of Reiki self-healing. I am grateful for the path that led me to Reiki. I believe that my life energy has been balanced for the greatest alignment of my mind, body, and soul.'

REIKI'S MOST COMMON FAQS AND MYTHS

FAQs

What is the Purpose of Learning Reiki?

There are several reasons to consider learning to practice Reiki on yourself. The ease of self-care is prized not just by people with health issues, but also by those with hectic schedules who want more balance in their life. It may assist both healthy persons and those suffering from chronic health illnesses—such as diabetes, asthma, cancer, epilepsy, fatigue syndromes, depression, or heart disease, to mention a few. They may use Reiki on themselves every day to ease stress and increase their well-being, and they can repeat the Reiki practice as frequently as they need to.

Daily Reiki self-care allows you to rebalance your life, alleviate stress, and reconnect with your sense of well-being.

Additionally, if required, bursts of Reiki practice throughout the day may provide centering and relief from pain, worry, and tension. People who learn Reiki self-care for anxiety or pain have the extra empowerment of knowing they are never again alone and powerless in their suffering.

There is also some anecdotal evidence that Reiki can assist animals in many of the same ways that people have. Those who practice Reiki on their dogs are often pleasantly surprised by their pets' interest and cooperation!

Lastly, when money is tight, the benefits of learning to practice

Reiki self-care versus paying for frequent treatments are evident. When a family member becomes unwell and it is no longer possible for the patient to self-treat, other members may provide Reiki and treat the patient (and other family members) and themselves.

What Should You Wear for a Reiki Session?

Wear clothing that allows you to relax. Wearing in layers may offer extra warmth and coziness. Before the session, remove any belts or other bulky items.

Can Reiki Really Heal My Ailment?

First and foremost, a difference must be drawn between healing and curing. Healing is the process of getting to the source of an issue and restoring the body's equilibrium. Curing is what is typically believed to be done when the issue is really gone (but maybe not the cause).

When you undergo surgery, you may remove the "sick" organ or tissue, but this may not fix the problem since the technique does not always address the underlying issue. It is also possible to be healed but not cured, which means that your body is in balance but you still have a medical condition.

There can be no guarantees concerning the outcome of using Reiki (or any other healing system, including conventional medicine). Everything is based on you, your intentions, your history, and the nature of the issue. Healing is a rewarding experience that has a unique impact on each person.

Recognizing your need for healing is a huge step in healing yourself.

What does Reiki Feel Like?

A Reiki session is a one-of-a-kind experience for each person, yet you may experience specific feelings when performing Reiki. To mention a few, common feelings include heat, tingling, pulsating, and freezing. Some folks have no feeling at all. Sensations, or their lack, merely reflect the individual's sensitivity to energy. Reiki flows whether you are aware of it or not.

What Happens Following a Reiki Session?

After the session, you may feel more sleepy than normal. This is not seen as a negative response, but as the body's natural healing response, which should be respected. People often express a sensation of peace and mental clarity, as well as a good night's sleep, after having Reiki.

Are There Any Side Effects to the Practice?

A Reiki treatment would usually leave a person feeling calm and energized. However, every now and then, a person will experience what is known as a healing crisis. Toxins stored in the body are released into the bloodstream when a person's vibration rises, where they are filtered by the liver and kidneys and eliminated from the system. When this occurs, a person may have a headache, stomach discomfort, or weakness. If this occurs, it is recommended that you drink more water, consume lighter meals, and get more rest. This is a healthy sign since the body is detoxifying as part of the healing process.

Who is Suitable to Practice Reiki?

Reiki is simple to learn and practice as self-care by anybody interested, regardless of age or condition. Children, as well as the elderly and infirm, may learn to practice. To begin learning, no prior background or certificates are required.

It is easy and requires no previous expertise in healing, meditation, or any other kind of training. Over one million individuals from all walks of life, young and old, have successfully mastered it. The reason it is so simple to learn is that it is not taught in the traditional manner.

With consistent practice and surrender, one may learn to do Reiki, and then anytime one lays their hands on oneself or another person to perform Reiki, the healing energy flows effortlessly.

Is There Anybody Who Should Stay Away from Reiki?

No. It's a gentle therapy that's suited for everyone, even newborns and the elderly.

How does Reiki Accurately Reveal Our True Self?

When we begin to recollect our True Self, we may get overwhelmed. The more we practice the Reiki system, the closer we get to self-actualization, enlightenment, remembering our True Self, and unity with the cosmos. This union with the cosmos may release a huge amount of power inside us; envision yourself as the universe and the universe as you, with no beginning or end!

In fact, Reiki practitioners are merely scratching the surface of what we are capable of realizing—such as union with the cosmos.

It is a shock to abruptly tap into these deeper levels, and our bodies may begin to tremble, or we may have bizarre visual experiences, intense pain, a sensation of loss of self, or emotions that we are without a body.

When this occurs, it is common for practitioners to feel hesitant, if not outright afraid. We may blame the energy for being excessive or painful. The fact is that this occurs because we are unprepared, that we have not laid the groundwork to gradually grow our inner power.

However, do not blame the "Kundalini" but blame the stupidity or incorrect techniques. Thus, to recall our True Self via the practice of the Reiki method, we must begin with the basics.

When we have properly prepared ourselves, the events will not be overpowering. Even if the sensations are rather intense, we will be able to cope with them because we have laid a firm foundation and prepared ourselves to encounter these deeper aspects of our True Self.

How does Reiki Healing Work on a Biological Level?

Over 50 trillion cells make up the human body. Each cell possesses all-knowing wisdom and is linked to the cosmos and all living things within it. Consider the cosmos to be a vast ocean of water. Every living creature in the ocean is as little as a droplet. These droplets combine to form and are a component of Reiki, the universal life energy.

Reiki is a part of our genetic make-up. An intellect that is built into the body, mind, and soul. Reiki promotes development, health, and vitality, as well as healing. When it is freely allowed to circulate throughout the body, it can keep us alive and healthy for more than a century.

Unfortunately, unhealthy habits and poor decisions suffocate the flow of Reiki. It is critical to understand that Reiki cannot be destroyed. Even when we die and our life energy departs from our bodies, we continue to exist as a part of the cosmos. We mistreat this fundamental component of life by neglect and ignorance.

When the mind, body, and spirit are in sync, the biological intelligence that manages the body's resources and enables it to recover and operate properly is magnified. Reiki is the key that unlocks the body's full potential.

The therapy boosts the immune system and the body's inherent healing capacities. Normally, the body will start by ridding itself of toxins. The body is rebalanced when the toxins are eliminated, and the healing process may begin.

How to Incorporate Reiki into Your Yoga Practice?

Because yoga involves channeling and using Prana, merging the two techniques makes logic. Certain 'opener' poses—such as Pigeon or Camel, also help to unblock energy, allowing it to flow and escape.

There are several methods to include Reiki into your yoga practice at any time. If you want to experience Reiki during class, for example, you may do so by breathing light and universal energy into your body. Send energy into the gaps while you do postures and holds. You may also use Ujjayi Breath to direct warm energy to particular points throughout your holds.

If you're a trainer, you may have your students do Yin or Restorative Yoga while also performing Reiki on them while they hold their postures. During Savasana, you might also place your hands on the shoulders and feet of your pupils to give them energy and anchor them. However, before touching or doing any therapeutic treatment on the person, you must first have their consent.

Is It Safe for Pregnant Women to Use?

Reiki can only be beneficial! Because Reiki is led by the Higher Power, the energy will recognize the client's or student's situation and modify accordingly. Many pregnant women have benefited from it. It is beneficial to both them and their unborn child. Reiki is also found to help with childbirth.

What is It Like to Provide a Treatment?

The Reiki energy goes through the practitioner before leaving the hands and entering the client during a Reiki session. As a result, the practitioner gets therapy as well. The practitioner will feel calmer and more elevated as the Reiki energy pours through her/him. Spiritual encounters do occur from time to time. Sometimes the practitioner gets insights into what the client needs to know in order to heal better.

Is Reiki Exhausting for the Practitioner?

No! Giving a treatment may be just as energizing as getting one. We're not utilizing our own energy, and we're not diagnosing or directing it either. We are merely letting this Universal Life Energy pass through us and into the receiver, where it will be most useful. However, the person providing must ensure that they are physically comfortable since they have to stay motionless in each posture for some time.

Can Reiki Aid Those Who have been Subjected to Black Magic?

Yes! Reiki cleanses your aura and protects against bad energies of all types—including the effects of black magic. It may also protect you from evil spirits.

Myths

Reiki is a form of Massage

Massage therapy and Reiki are two independent fields. Although many massage therapists include Reiki healing in their massage sessions, Reiki is NOT a massage therapy. It is an energy-based treatment that does not entail bone or tissue manipulation. Healers employ a gentle touch with their hands on their bodies or over the completely clothed bodies of their guests.

Reiki is a New-Age Practice with No Scientific Basis

Skeptics dismiss Reiki as a joke or something that isn't founded on scientific evidence. Although research is restricted compared to Western medicine, there is an increasing amount of data showing the benefits of Reiki and other energy healing methods on the human body.

According to these researches, it decreases the negative effects of medications and medical procedures, and it may even protect healthy cells from radiation therapy. It also relaxes stress, decreases blood pressure, heart rate, and breathing rates, relieves pain and discomfort, reduces bleeding, increases red blood cell count, and aids in the treatment of insomnia. These are only a handful of the studied advantages of energy healing.

It is a Very Complicated Practice

False. Reiki is not magic. It is not a gift conferred upon a select few. Reiki energy is, in fact, available to everybody and everyone. You just got to have the courage to expose yourself to it. Although Reiki energy is present in everyone, to use the Reiki approach therapeutically, one must be dedicated.

Reiki is Capable of Curing Anything

Reiki isn't a cure for everything. It instead aids in the induction of relaxation response and the promotion of a mind-body balance favorable to healing. Curing entails addressing the physical reasons of a health disease as well as the symptoms. Reiki healing includes spiritual, emotional, and mental unblocking and re-balancing to help get to the core cause of a problem, getting back on track, and creating an ideal environment for the body to recover.

The Benefits of Reiki are Instantly Felt

Yes, there is instant relaxation and tranquillity, but Reiki's healing effect continues beyond a single therapy session, and it helps cleanse bad energy and make way for development in the long run.

Reiki promotes healing, and healing is a process that must be repeated over time to deliver effects.

Symbols are the Energy

Some newer variants of the Reiki method keep adding symbols

to acquire more energy. They get hooked on the notion of themselves and need more and more to become what they feel they are not—'powerful.' This is due to the false belief that symbols represent the energy itself.

Everything has energy, and the Reiki system works with that energy. Energy cannot be confined; it cannot be placed in a box.

By claiming that the symbols represent energy, you are implying that they are like a magic wand. This is an external perspective on life, one that looks for factors outside to alter ourselves and our circumstances. It takes away our self-responsibility—the basic foundation of the Reiki system.

Only we can bring about the change we want in our life; they must originate from inside.

Nothing is Happening If You Don't Feel Anything

So, here's the deal, when people first get introduced to the power of Reiki, there's generally a lot of enthusiasm about the instant feelings that occur.

These include the extremely tangible sense of Reiki radiating from their hands, which results in the Reiki "hot hands" phenomena; their enhanced sensitivity to the status of one's chakras (theirs and others'); and the experience of energy flowing through their bodies.

Not to mention the incredible energy experiences that individuals often experience during a good Reiki healing session.

Don't get me wrong, I like these feelings as well! But that is NOT the case with Reiki.

Reiki, as an energy healing approach, focuses on the subtle body, which includes your spiritual body, aura, and energetic body. As a result, its effects are energetic in nature, and depending on one's present condition, physical and emotional manifestations of Reiki healing may occur immediately or very quickly after

Reiki has been transmitted.

Whether someone is experiencing these physical or emotional feelings at any one moment is determined by a variety of circumstances—including their present mental state, physical health, energy levels, mood, and whether or not they are feeling especially blocked.

Reiki is effective in any case. Reiki works, whether you feel the results right away or not. In fact, it's important to realize that Reiki's effects are far-reaching and work with you over time; so, just because you had an instant reaction or feeling doesn't imply it's the end of it. Reiki will continue to assist you for as long as you need it.

Another thing to consider is that most individuals experience the least degree of visceral feeling while practicing Reiki on themselves. There are several theories for this, but the one that resonates with me the most is that we have such high expectations of ourselves and our outcomes that we subconsciously stop ourselves from receiving. You'll become more sensitive to the healing feelings during your Reiki practice as you learn to relax and surrender to the experience.

Finally, pushing Reiki to flow will have the opposite impact you want. If you felt nothing at first and then continue to push Reiki mentally, you'll build the largest mental and energy block ever and frustrate yourself. Surrendering to the Reiki energy is the way to go. Don't worry! The Reiki will flow, and you'll get healing on a subtle level. But pushing Divine energy will not get you anywhere.

Giving Reiki to Others will Deplete MY ENERGY

Please keep in mind that Reiki has no recorded negative effects on either the practitioner or the recipient. A Reiki practitioner does not provide the receiver with his or her own energy. As a result, there is nothing to deplete.

In Reiki, we direct energy from the source to the receiver through our body. We essentially deliver mail. When the mailman delivers the Reiki delivery, he returns home in one piece.

What happens next is entirely up to the package and the receiver! The recipient's body takes what it needs from the healer's hands, absorbing and using it.

However, a Reiki practitioner can get fatigued while or after treating someone. But Reiki has been wrongfully accused. If this occurs, it suggests that something is out of balance in their own body, or that they have inadvertently absorbed energy from the client. They should return it since it does not belong to them!

Reiki will Permanently Heal Me

Reiki is not a magic pill. True, a Reiki session may result in magnificent permanent healing, but some conditions may need several sessions, particularly if the receiver has poor habits—such as negative self-talk, or lives in a bad environment.

Reiki healing is not a medication. Instead, it treats both the causes and the symptoms. It is a holistic healing approach that works with the body's natural cycles and processes to repair the problem in its own time and manner.

Reiki is a Religion or Cult

The term 'Reiki' means 'Spiritual Energy.' Reiki is a system of energy that pervades everything—birds, rocks, your beating heart, halloumi cheese. Everything is comprised of energy.

While Reiki is a spiritual practice, it is not affiliated with any religion or cult. There are no Reiki churches, priests, sermons, or memberships. There will also be no commune of Reiki initiates who enthusiastically follow and give all of their money to their Reiki masters. Reiki practitioners are independent thinkers, not followers.

Even the guiding concepts that serve as the core of Reiki are not religious in nature. Reiki is, by definition, a practice—even an art form.

Reiki practice helps us to harness the energy and enables it to flow more easily in and through us. We progressively rediscover our true nature and embrace a more balanced, healthy, and joyful way of life.

It is a system, not a religion or a set of beliefs. It does not violate anyone's beliefs or personal values. People of all religions may benefit from it.

CLOSING WORDS

Reiki is a wonderful healing practice that fosters self-healing, personal empowerment, and overall well-being. It may serve as an inner anchor in your greatest, most expansive, eternal self, a reminder of who you really are, allowing you to live your life with gratitude, love, and creativity. However, these privileges demand patience, determination, and, most importantly, surrender.

Reiki energy is contained in everyone and is open to all! Even if you haven't been attuned to Reiki by any master, you can practice it. It just takes a little courage and dedication to show up for your own success. Starting your Reiki journey with a comfortable posture, meditation, recitation of the Reiki principles, and hands-on healing is a good place to start. You can then work your way up to symbols, crystals, and distance healing.

Make sure you set some time each day for yourself to practice Reiki. You can be certain that the results will be evident. Just for today, do not anger, do not worry, be grateful, expand your consciousness, and be compassionate to yourself and others. If you go about your day with the Principles in your heart, you will shed your light on everyone you meet, which will help you attract abundance in your practice.

Finally, I wish you all the luck and success as you embark on this healing journey...

AUTHOR NOTE

So, I think I've been able to provide you with a deeper insight on Reiki. Thank you for reading one of my books! This is the 32nd book I've written since 2018. It took me a long time to write my first book, mostly because I was new to the writing world and has very little knowledge of how to publish books.

I thought my first book will be a Bestseller, but as you may guess it didn't go well, in fact, I got a negative review on it by the 3rd reader itself. I learned a lot over time and still learning something new every day. And as I am on this journey, I realized that writing books is a great way to reach people around the world and share some valuable knowledge.

Moreover, I enjoy writing books, books that can help people to be content, happy, and healthy in all aspects of well-being (Mind, Body, and Soul). It may sound idiotic, but I've left my full-time job just to write books more efficiently.

Why am I telling you all this?? Because I think it's important that readers should know their value. You can give your review on books, trust me that's a superpower! Not just authors, but you too add value to a book. Referring to your reviews, a reader decides whether or not to invest in that book. You can make or break the journey of a book, that's your power!

Your review is extremely valuable to me. I really want to know what you think of my books. No, I'm not manipulating you to give me a 5-star review, you're free to judge. Just don't go without leaving a review! It'll help others get a better idea of the book. For me, it'll motivate me towards writing and improving more.

So please share your meaningful review of this book! Here's the link that'll take you directly to the review section- Click Here

Once again thanks for reading…

You can lend this book to your family, it's free of cost!!

You can also contact me for any queries: rohit@rohitsahu.net or on any of the following social media:

Facebook, Twitter, Instagram, Goodreads, Linkedin: Rohit Sahu

HERE'S YOUR FREE GIFT!!

If you're into Chakras and pursuing knowledge about Chakras Awakening and Vibrational Energy, this book will help you pave the way towards your spiritual growth. You can also join the mailing list to be the first to hear new release updates, improved recommendations, and bonus content.

Being on my email list means you'll be the first to know when I release a new book. I plan to release them at a steep discount (or even FREE) for the first 24 hours. By signing up for my list, you'll get early notifications. And if you don't want to join my list, it's totally fine. It just means that I just need to earn your trust.

CLICK HERE to Claim The Book!! or follow this link- https://bit.ly/chakrasforbeginners

CLICK HERE to Join My Mailing List or follow this link if this is a paperback- http://bit.ly/theMailingList

BOOKS BY THIS AUTHOR

Ayurveda For Beginners (3 Book Series)

Ayurveda, which derives from ancient Vedic scriptures, is a 5,000-year-old medical ideology and philosophy based on the idea that we are all made up of different types of energy.

There are three Doshas in Ayurveda that describe the dominant state of mind/body: Vata, Pitta, and Kapha. While all three are present in everyone, Ayurveda suggests that we each have a dominant Dosha that is unwavering from birth, and ideally an equal (though often fluctuating) balance between the other two.

If Doshas are balanced, we are healthy; when they are unbalanced, we develop a disorder commonly expressed by skin problems, impaired nutrition, insomnia, irritability, and anxiety.

Vata, Pitta, and Kapha are all important to our biology in some way, so no one is greater than, or superior to, any other. Each has a very specific set of basic functions to perform in the body.

That said, when the Doshas are out of control, our wellbeing can be damaged. However, before we get into the particulars of each of the three Doshas, it is helpful to understand their basic nature and their wider function in the natural world.

Each of the Doshas has its own special strengths and weaknesses, and with a little awareness, you can do a lot to remain healthy and balanced. You can use this series to adjust your lifestyles and routines in a way that supports your constitution.

I've made a complete series of these three.

Just follow the books along, you'll reveal the easiest step-by-step routine to balance your Dosha by the end of it!

Ayurveda Cookbook For Beginners (3 Book Series)

All you need to know about Ayurvedic diet and cooking along with easy-to-follow recipes backed by the timeless wisdom of Indian heritage to balance your aggravated dosha...

I've made a complete cookbook series on all 3 doshas! You can use this series to adjust your lifestyles and routines in a way that supports your constitution.

With this "Ayurveda Cookbook For Beginners Series," I provide you the best dietary practices, recipes, and everything you need to balance and heal your doshas alongside enjoying the authentic Indian flavors.

This guide's Ayurvedic Cooking techniques tell what to eat and how to eat to help the healing process and assist the body in removing contaminants and maintaining equilibrium. It has a wealth of knowledge on healthy diet, proper food combinations, food quality, food timing, and cooking methods.

All the recipes in this cookbook are traditional, time-tested over decades, and are based on Ayurvedic principles. They can aid a yogi's yoga practice by keeping the mind calm and are thus ideal for all yoga practitioners. The beauty is that the recipes are not only sattvic in nature but are also tasty and have that authentic Indian taste!

Yoga For Beginners (10 Book Series)

Yoga origin can be traced back to more than 5,000 years ago, but some researchers believe that yoga may be up to 10,000 years old. The word 'Yoga' first appeared in the oldest sacred texts, the Rig Veda, and is derived from the Sanskrit root "Yuj" which means to unite.

According to the Yoga Scriptures, the practice of yoga leads an individual to a union of consciousness with that of universal consciousness. It eventually leads to a great harmony between the human mind and body, man, and nature.

Yoga provides multiple health advantages, such as enhancing endurance, reducing depression, and improving overall wellness and fitness.

As yoga has grown into mainstream popularity, many styles and variations have emerged in wellness space. This centuries-old Eastern philosophy is now widely practiced and taught by people of all ages, sizes, and backgrounds.

There are 10 primary types of Yoga. So if you're trying to figure out which of the different types of Yoga is best for you, remember that there's no one right or wrong. You can ask yourself what's important to you in your Yoga practice: Are you searching for a sweaty, intense practice, or are you searching for a more meditative, gentler practice that looks more appealing?

Like you choose any sort of exercise, choose something you want to do.

Here's a complete series on all 10 types of yoga.

This guide can be used by beginners, advanced students,

teachers, trainees, and teacher training programs. Covering the fundamentals of each pose in exact detail, including how to correct the most common mistakes, as well as changes to almost all body types, this yoga guides has left nothing to help you make daily breakthroughs.

Vipassana Meditation: The Buddhist Mindfulness Practice To Cultivate Joy, Peace, Calmness, And Awakening!!

Are you looking to cultivate true unconditional love towards the creation and experience utter bliss? Do you wish to foster resilience, non-judgment, and detachment? Will you like to master the ancient mindfulness technique that leaded Gautama Buddha to Enlightenment/Nirvana? Do you want to promote relaxation, mindfulness, gratitude, and a better sense of inner peace? Do you want to witness the joy of living in the present moment? If so, Vipassana Meditation is what you need...

Vipassana, which means "seeing things as they really are," is an Indian and Buddhist meditation practice. It was taught over 2500 years ago as a generic cure for universal maladies, i.e., an Art of Living. It is a simple knowledge of what is happening as it is happening.

It is distinct from other forms of meditation practices. The bulk of meditations, whether on a mantra, flame, or activity such as Trataka, are focused on concentration. The practitioner directs his mental energy on an item or a concept. Such methods have validity in terms of relaxing the mind, relaxation, a feeling of well-being, stress reduction, and so on.

Vipassana, in contrast to the other practices, focuses on awareness rather than concentration. Vipassana refers to perceiving reality as it is rather than changing reality, as in concentration practices. The key attribute of Vipassana is its secular nature, which allows it to be practiced by people of any religion, race, caste, nationality, or gender. If the method is to be universal, it must be used by everyone. Here, you concentrate on your breathing, and as you gain control of your breathing observation, you move on to your body responses.

The more the method is used, the more freedom from suffering there is, and the closer one gets to the ultimate objective of complete liberation. Even 10 days may provide effects that are apparent and clearly helpful in daily life.

This step-by-step Vipassana guide takes the reader through practices that may open new levels of awareness and understanding. This book's aim is to teach you how to live consciously so that you may ultimately be calm and joyful every day of your life!

This is an authentic and practical guide to samatha, materialism, mind, dependent origination, and Vipassana based on the Buddha's teachings. This book will walk you through the stages and methods of overcoming stress, sadness, fear, and anxiety through the practice of Vipassana meditation.

It will explain what this method is and how it came to be. This book also demonstrates how to utilize Vipassana meditation to make our everyday lives more meaningful and, ultimately, to discover the real meaning of peace and tranquillity.

In this book, you'll discover:
✓ History of Vipassana Meditation
✓ The Deeper Realm of Vipassana
✓ The Purpose of Vipassana
✓ The Benefits of Vipassana Meditation
✓ The Right Attitude Towards the Practice
✓ How to Create a Vipassana Retreat at Home

✓The Step-By-Step Vipassana Meditation Practice
✓Tips to Boost Your Progress
✓Additions to Catalyze Your Vipassana Session
✓Beginners Mistakes
✓Common Myths and FAQs
✓Some Pointers from My Experience

Following the instructions in this book will teach you how to develop profound stability, maintain an in-depth study of the intricacies of mind and matter, and ultimately unravel deeply conditioned patterns that perpetuate suffering. It acknowledges with a detailed examination of the different insight and spiritual fruits that the practice offers, Nirvana/Enlightenment being the end goal.

Aromatherapy To Foster Health, Beauty, Healing, And Well-Being!!

Do you want to fill your home with calming essence and the pleasant smell of nature? Do you wish to get rid of stress and anxiety and relieve various physical and mental conditions? Are you looking to improve your overall physical, mental, emotional, and spiritual health? Do you wish to escalate your spiritual practices? If so, Aromatherapy is what you need…

Even though the word "Aromatherapy" was not coined until the late 1920s, this kind of therapy was found many centuries earlier. The history of the use of essential oils traces back to at least a few thousand years, although human beings have used plants, herbs, etc. for thousands of years. They have been used to improve a person's health or mood for over 6,000 years. Its roots may be traced back to ancient Egypt when fragrant compounds like frankincense and myrrh were utilized in religious and spiritual rituals.

Aromatherapy, often known as essential oil treatment, refers to a group of traditional, alternative, and complementary therapies that make use of essential oils and other aromatic plant components. It is a holistic therapeutic therapy that promotes health and well-being by using natural plant extracts. It employs the therapeutic use of fragrant essential oils to enhance the health of the body, mind, and soul.

Various techniques are used to extract essential or volatile oils from the plant's flowers, bark, stems, leaves, roots, fruits, and other components. It arose as a result of scientists deciphering the antibacterial and skin permeability characteristics of essential oils.

In the modern world, aromatherapy and essential oils have become increasingly popular, not only in the usage of aromatherapy massage and the purchase of pure essential oils but also in the extensive use of essential oils in the cosmetic, skincare, and pharmaceutical industries. Aromatherapy is considered both an art and a science. It provides a variety of medical and psychological advantages, depending on the essential oil or oil combination and manner of application employed.

With this book, I'll share with you every aspect of aromatherapy, as well as the finest techniques you may use to reap the physical, mental, emotional, and spiritual benefits.

This book brings light to the world of aromatherapy by offering a wealth of knowledge and practical guidance on how to get the most out of essential oils. It will offer the best option for living a joyful, natural, healthy, and homeopathic way of life. You will discover a variety of information on the best aromatherapy oils on these pages, including benefits, tips, applications, precautions, myths, and FAQs for using them safely and effectively.

You will discover the science of aromatherapy and how essential oils may totally change your well-being by using the methods mentioned. This book will help you use these potent plant extracts to start feeling better inside and out, no matter where you are on your aromatherapy self-care journey.

In this book, you'll discover:
✓What is Aromatherapy?
✓History and its Significance
✓Aromatherapy Benefits and Conditions it may Treat
✓What are Essential Oils?
✓How are Essential oils Made?
✓The Best Storage Procedure
✓How to Buy Quality Essential Oils?
✓The Best Way to Perform Aromatherapy
✓Activities to perform with Aromatherapy
✓Some Tips that'll Boost Your Progress
✓Essential Oils to Avoid
✓Safety and Precautions
✓Myths and FAQs

So, if you are interested in healing with minimum medication use, spending your time learning about essential oils is a good place to start. Just stick with me until the end to discover how this becomes your ultimate aromatherapy reference and the manifestation of your motives.

The Ayurvedic Dinacharya: Master Your Daily Routine As Per Ayurveda For A Healthy Life And Well-Being!!

Do you wish to synchronize your schedule with nature's rhythm? Do you wish to be disease-free for the rest of your life? Do you want to live a longer, better, and happier life? If yes, this book is going to be an important asset in your life...

Our generation is usually always going through a tough phase. Late nights at work, early meetings, and hectic social life are just a few things that add to our everyday stress. But the main cause for your distress is the lack of a regular schedule. Our forefathers never had to worry about stress since they maintained a disciplined Dinacharya that they followed faithfully. This helps keep the doshas in balance, controls the body's biological cycle, promotes discipline and happiness, and reduces stress.

A lack of routine can also cause many lifestyle disorders such as obesity, hypertension and stroke, diabetes, coronary heart disease, dyslipidemia, cancer, arthritis, anxiety, insomnia, constipation, indigestion, hyperacidity, gastric ulcer, and early manifestations of aging like greying of hair, wrinkles, depletion of energy levels, etc. Simple adjustments in one's lifestyle may prevent these numerous health risks and more.

Dinacharya is formed from two words—'Dina,' which means day, and 'Acharya,' which means activity. By incorporating Dinacharya's basic self-care practices into your life, you will be armed with the skills you need to foster balance, joy, and overall long-term health. It teaches people how to live a better, happier, and longer life while avoiding any illnesses. So irrespective of your body type, age, gender, or health condition, you should opt for a healthy lifestyle.

A daily routine is essential for bringing about a dramatic transformation in the body, mind, and consciousness. Routine aids in the establishment of equilibrium in one's constitution. It also helps with digestion, absorption, and assimilation, as well as generating self-esteem, discipline, tranquility, happiness, and longevity.

With this book, I'll show you how to align yourself with nature's rhythm every day so you may remain healthy and happy for the rest of your life. You will overcome all kinds of mental and physical illnesses in your life. The best part is that these suggestions are centered on Ayurvedic principles and are easy to implement.

This book covers:
✓What is Dinacharya?
✓Importance of Dinacharya
✓Dinacharya Benefits
✓Daily Cycles and Dinacharya
✓The Morning Dinacharya
✓The Afternoon and Sundown Dinacharya
✓The Evening and Night Dinacharya
✓How to Implement Dinacharya into Your Life?
✓Tips to Boost Your Progress
✓Beginners Dinacharya Mistakes

This book is perfect for anybody seeking simple, all-encompassing methods to live a more genuine and balanced life. You'll discover techniques and ideas to help you stay calm, balanced, and joyful.

Shadow Work For Beginners: A Short And Powerful Guide To Make Peace With Your Hidden Dark Side That Drive You And Illuminate The Hidden Power Of Your True Self For Freedom And Lasting Happiness

Do you want to recognize and heal the shadow patterns and wounds of your inner child? Do you wish to get rooted in your soul for wholeness? Do you want to influence your programs and beliefs to attain eternal bliss? Do you want to know where you are on the ladder of consciousness, and how to move up? Do you want to learn how to forgive, let go, and have compassion for yourself and others? Do you want to alter and strengthen your mindset to maximize every aspect of your life? If so, this guide is just what you need.

For many, the word "shadow work" conjures up all sorts of negative and dark ideas. Because of the beliefs we have of the term shadow, it is tempting to believe that shadow work is a morbid spiritual practice or that it is an internal work that includes the more destructive or evil facets of our personalities. But that's not the case. In fact, shadow work is vital to your spiritual growth. When you go through a spiritual awakening, there comes a point where "shadow work" becomes necessary. So, what exactly is the 'Human Shadow,' and what is 'Shadow Work?'

The definition of the shadow self is based on the idea that we figuratively bury certain bits of personality that we feel will not be embraced, approved, or cherished by others; thus, we hold them in the "shadows." In brief, our shadows are the versions of ourselves that we do not offer society.

It includes aspects of our personality that we find shameful, unacceptable, ugly. It may be anger, resentment, frustration, greed, hunger for strength, or the wounds of childhood—all those we hold secret. You might claim it's the dark side of yourself. And no matter what everyone suggests, they all have a dark side of their personalities.

Shadow Work is the practice of loving what is, and of freeing shame and judgment, so that we can be our true self in order to touch the very depths of our being, that is what Shadow Work means. You have to dwell on the actual problems rather than on past emotions. If you do so, you get to the problems that have you stressed out instantly and easily. And to be at peace, we need to get in touch with our darker side, rather than suppressing it.

Whether you have struggled with wealth, weight, love, or something else, after dissolving the shadows within, you will find that your life is transforming in both tiny and drastic ways. You'll draw more optimistic people and better opportunities.

Your life will be nicer, easier, and even more abundant.

The book covers the easiest practices and guided meditation to tap into the unconscious. It's going to help you explore certain aspects so that they will no longer control your emotions. Just imagine what it would be if you could see challenges as exciting obstacles rather than experiencing crippling anxiety.

This book is going to be the Momentum you need to get to where you're trying to be. You'll go deeper into your thoughts, the beliefs that hold you back disappear, and you get a head start on your healing journey.

In this guide, you'll discover:

✓What is the Human Shadow?
✓Characteristics of Shadow
✓Do We All Have a Shadow Self?
✓How is The Shadow Born?
✓What is the Golden Shadow?
✓The Mistake We All Make
✓What is Shadow Work?
✓Benefits of Shadow Work
✓Tips on Practicing Shadow Work
✓Shadow Work Stages
✓Shadow Work Techniques and Practices
✓Shadow Work Mindfulness
✓Shadow Work FAQs

Covering every bit of Shadow Work, this guide will subtly reveal the root of your fear, discomfort, and suffering, showing you that when you allow certain pieces of yourself to awaken and be, you will eventually begin to recover, transcend your limits, and open yourself to the light and beauty of your true existence.

Spiritual Empath: The Ultimate Guide To Awake Your Maximum Capacity And Have That Power, Compassion, And Wisdom Contained In Your Soul

Do you keep attracting toxic individuals and set a poor barrier? Do you get consumed by negative emotions and feel like you can't deal with it? Do you want to heal yourself and seek inner peace and spiritual growth? If so, this book is going to open the doors for you!!

Empaths have too much to contribute as healers, creators, friends, lovers, and innovators at work. Yet extremely compassionate and empathic people sometimes give too much at the cost of their own well-being-and end up consuming the stress of others. Why?

These questions and more will be addressed in this book. You'll find the answers you're searching for to learn the facts on whether you're an empath, how it can work on a biological level, what to do to help you succeed as an empath, and how to shield yourself from other people's thoughts, feelings, and responses so that you don't absorb them.

There is a lot of things going in the life of empaths, and they are here to add more happiness and peace to the world. Empaths are known for their willingness to listen, sensitivity, empathy, and the capacity to be in the shoes of others. You may be that individual, or you might know that individual in your life, but either way, knowing the true cause of being an empath and why they are different from others will help you improve to lead a healthy, free, and beautiful life full of empathy.

This book includes the following, and much more:

✓What is an Empath?
✓Are You an Empath?
✓Is Being an Empath a Gift or Disorder
✓The List of Empath Superpowers
✓Ways to Turn Your Super Traits into Super Powers
✓The Secret Dark Side of Being an Empath
✓What It's Like Being an Intuitive/Psychic Empath
✓Signs You're the Most Powerful Empath (Heyoka)
✓Is Your Soul Exhausted and Energy Depleted?
✓Tips To Become an Empath Warrior
✓Empath's Survival Guide/Tips to Stay Balanced as an Empath
✓Ways to Save Yourself from Narcissists
✓Best Practices to Deal with Anxiety
✓Why Self-Love/Self-Care is So Important
✓Empath Awakening Stages
✓Best Transmutation Techniques for Raising Your Energies and Vibrations for Spiritual Growth

Right now, you can opt to proceed on a profound healing path and find strength in the deep pockets of your soul. Or you might want to put off the re-discovery of your inner voice and intuition, feeling like you might never have had it; never really understood how your powerful empathic ability can be channeled for the greatest benefit of all, including your own highest gain.

Filled with lots of insight into the inner workings of Empath's mind, useful knowledge to help you make sense of your abilities, and keep negative individuals and energies out of your life. This book contains all you need to become a stronger, better version of yourself.

That's correct, with this book, you can move out of your usual role and begin a journey. You'll experience the emergence of the inner energies and become a spiritually awakened person.

Meditation For Beginners: The Easiest Guide To Cultivate Awareness, Acceptance, And Peace To Unleash Your Inner Strength And Explore The Deepest Realm Of Your Being!!

Whether you're looking to increase self-awareness, reduce negative emotions, bust stress, promote creativity, foster good health and mental peace, or transcend the limitations of human life and connect with universal forces to see the transcendental reality through it (called Brahman in the Vedas), meditation solves all...

It is estimated that 200–500 million individuals meditate across the globe. Meditation statistics suggest that the practice has grown in popularity in recent years. Given all the health advantages it provides, it's no wonder that a rising number of individuals are using it. Through it, more and more people are recognizing a profound inner longing for authenticity, connection, compassion, and aliveness.

Meditation may seem to be a simple concept—sit still, focus on your breath, and observe. However, the practice of meditation has a long cultural history that has seen it evolve from a religious concept to something that might today seem more alluring than spiritual. It is a centuries-old technique that is said to have started in India thousands of years ago. Throughout history, the practice was gradually adopted by neighboring nations and became a part of numerous religions around the globe.

The goal of meditation is to become consciously aware of or explore one's own mind and body to get to know oneself. It is fundamentally both an exclusive and inclusive process in which one withdraws one's thoughts and senses from the distractions of the world and concentrates on a selected object or idea.

It is focused attention, with or without an individual's will, in which the mind and body must be brought together to work as one harmonic whole. We may overcome mental obstacles, negative thinking, crippling worries, tension, and anxiety with the aid of meditation by understanding and dealing with the underlying causes. We gain insightful awareness in meditation, allowing us to manage our responses and reactions.

So, whether you want to ease stress, attain spiritual enlightenment, seek peace, or flow through movement, meditation is the way to go.

But how will we know which meditation practice is best for us as there are plenty of them?? While there are various types of meditation, each takes you to the same spot. It's like there are various routes to the same destination. So, it didn't matter which route you take. Here in this book, I'll discuss a certain type of meditation that I found to be the easiest and most effective.

Although there is no right or incorrect method to meditate, it is important to select a practice that matches your requirements and compliments your nature. And the type of meditation I'm going to discuss here is ideal for anyone—from beginners to advanced.

The practice will inject far-reaching and long-lasting advantages into your life—lower stress, more awareness of your struggles, better ability to connect, enhanced awareness, and being nicer to yourself are just some of its benefits.

In this book, you'll discover:
✓What is Meditation?
✓Meditation Benefits
✓The Role of Diet in Meditation
✓Various Mudras

- ✓Various Asanas
- ✓The Ideal Setting for Meditation
- ✓How Yoga and Pranayamas can Help Boost the Practice?
- ✓The Easiest Meditation Practice
- ✓The Wrong Way to Approach Meditation
- ✓The Right Way to Approach Meditation
- ✓The Significance of Keeping the Spine Straight
- ✓The Importance of Breath Rhythm
- ✓Some Tips to Enhance the Practice
- ✓How Group Meditation is Better than Meditating Alone?
- ✓The Significance of Routine
- ✓How to Bring Meditation to Daily Life Activities?
- ✓Common Meditation Myths and FAQs
- ✓Some Tips from Experience

So, if you're ready, claim your copy right now and embark on this quest beyond yourself...

Who Are You: The Spiritual Awakening Self Discovery Guide For Enlightenment And Liberation

Have you ever thought after reaching your goal, why aren't you happy? It's because that is not what you need to be happy.

The major problem today in this world is that everyone is searching for joy in materialistic objects like money, fame, respect, and whatever. But the fact is, the most successful personalities in the world which you admire so much are not happy at all! If that was the case, they won't ever get depressed or sad. Is that what the reality is? No, in fact, they're the one who takes depression therapies and drugs to be happy.

What are all the fundamental problems that we all face? There is a sense of lack that exists in all of us, a sense of loneliness, a sense of incompleteness, a sense of being restricted, a sense of fear, fear of death. So these fundamental problems can only be overcome through self-investigation; there's no other way around.

Being happy is a basic nature of human beings, just like the basic nature of fire is hot. But the error we make is we're searching for happiness outside, which is impossible to achieve. Say, you wanted something for a very long time; what happens after you achieve it? You'll be happy for a while, but then you'll need something else to be happy, you'll then run after some other goal; it's an endless cycle!

The good thing is, there's a way to be happy at every moment, but to make it happen you must understand in a peaceful state of mind "Who Are You?"
You'll have to self-enquire! This book is based on one of the most popular Indian Scripture "Ashtavakra Geeta" that reveals the ultimate truth of mankind. It will open the doors for you on how we can achieve self-knowledge and be fearless. All your fears and doubts will come to an end; not temporarily, but forever. All internal conflicts will fall to zero, and psychological pain will cease to exist.

This is not just another self-help book; this spiritual workbook will help you achieve liberation and be self-enlightened!

Reading this book:
✓You'll attain everlasting peace
✓You'll understand the real meaning of spiritual awakening
✓You'll understand spirituality over religion
✓You'll get the answer to 'Who Are You?'
✓You'll be fearless
✓You'll be free from bondage and be able to achieve liberation
✓You'll get the key to everlasting happiness and joy
✓You'll grasp the real essence of spirituality and the awakening

self
✓You'll get to know about spirituality for the skeptic
✓You'll discover your higher self
✓You'll be able to experience the joy of self-realization
✓You'll find what spiritual enlightenment means in Buddhism
✓You'll know how to achieve or reach spiritual enlightenment
✓You'll know what happens after spiritual enlightenment
✓You'll get the answer to why you should have spiritual awakening

And this is a book not just for adults but also for kids and teens.

Chakras For Beginners: A Guide To Understanding 7 Chakras Of The Body: Nourish, Heal, And Fuel The Chakras For Higher Consciousness And Awakening! (Available For Free!!)

Chakras are the circular vortexes of energy that are placed in seven different points on the spinal column, and all the seven chakras are connected to the various organs and glands within the body. These chakras are responsible for disturbing the life energy, which is also known as Qi or Praana.

Chakras have more than one dimension to them. One dimension is their physical existence, but they also have a spiritual dimension. Whenever a chakra is disrupted or blocked, the life energy also gets blocked, leading to the onset of mental and health ailments. When the harmonious balance of the seven chakras is disrupted or damaged, it can cause several problems in our lives, including our physical health, emotional health, and our mental state of mind. If all our chakras are balanced and in harmony, our body will function in an optimum way; If unbalanced, our energies will be like in a small river where the water will flow irregularly and noisily. By balancing our chakras, the water/our energies will flow more freely throughout our bodies and thus the risk of imbalances and consequent illnesses will be reduced to a minimum.

In this book, I'm going to give you an excellent resource you can use to amplify the work you do with your chakras.

In this book you'll learn:

✓ The Number of Chakras in Our Body (Not 7)
✓ The Location of Chakras
✓ Meaning Related to Each Chakra
✓ Color Psychology
✓ How to Balance the Chakras
✓ Characteristics/Impacts of Each Chakra When Balanced and Imbalanced
✓ Aspects of Nature
✓ Qualities
✓ Gemstones to Support Each Chakra

Step-By-Step Beginners Instant Pot Cookbook (Vegan): 100+ Easy, Delicious Yet Extremely Healthy Instant Pot Recipes Backed By Ayurveda Which Anyone Can Make In Less Than 30 Minutes

Who said healthy foods can't be tasty, I am a health-conscious person and love to eat healthy food, as well as tasty food.

"You Don't Have to Cook Fancy or Complicated Masterpieces. Just Tasty Food From Simple Healthy Ingredients."

Well, you don't have to struggle anymore with the taste. Here in this cookbook, you'll find 100+ easy yet extremely delicious instant pot recipes. keeping in mind the health factor, all these recipes are backed by Ayurveda, so yes, all are highly nutritious as well.

If you follow Ayurveda you know why we shouldn't eat meat or non-veg, so finally here is a Complete Vegan Instant Pot Cookbook. Plus, these do not require ingredients that'll hurt your budget, nearly all the ingredients are readily available in your home.

Every recipe is properly portioned and will be ready in 30 minutes or less. These quick and simple recipes will get your meal ready on the table in no time.

In this Instant Pot Cookbook you will find:

✓ Insider's Knowledge on How to Make the Most Out of Your Instant Pot
✓ Common FAQs and Other Must-Know Facts about Your Instant Pot
✓ Pro Tips to Get the Most out of Your Instant pot
✓ Things Not to Do with Your Instant Pot
✓ No Non-Veg, Complete Vegan Recipes
✓ How to Create a Variety of Healthy, Easy-to-Make, Delicious Recipes in the Easiest Way Possible

No matter if you're a solo eater, or if you cook for the whole family or friends, with these easy and healthy recipes, you can surprise your family, friends, and your loved ones.

This cookbook includes delicious recipes for:

✓Breakfast Meals
✓Stews and Chilies
✓Soups
✓Beans
✓Lunch/Brunch
✓Side Meals

- ✓Main Course Meals
- ✓Appetizers & Snacks
- ✓Light Dinner
- ✓Deserts
- ✓Bonus Recipes Including Salads, Drinks, and Some of the Most Popular Indian Dishes

Made in the USA
Middletown, DE
29 April 2023